The Sword of the Spirit

Prayers Against Spiritual Warfare Attacks

Richard W. Allen

WHAT IS THE BASIC BIBLE SERIES

Welcome to the *Basic Bible Series*, a collection of essential guides designed to equip Christians with the foundational truths of our faith. The word "basic" implies that the series intends to cover the basics of Christianity that all believers should know about in their walk with God. It does not imply that the book has basic surface-level knowledge, it is far from that! Each book delves into a core element of Christianity, drawing directly from Scripture to illuminate its relevance for everyday life.

Whether you're just beginning your walk with Christ or have been journeying for years, these volumes provide clear, biblically grounded insights to strengthen your relationship with God and empower you to live out your faith authentically. My goal is to make the profound truths of the Bible accessible and the *Basic Bible Series* is an invitation to transformation. God doesn't want us merely informed; He longs for us to be conformed to the image of His Son. Let each book inspire you to go deeper in your faith. As you read, pray for wisdom to understand, discuss these truths with fellow believers, and apply them to your life. The fruits will follow. May these 90 powerful prayers across 20 evil spirits mentioned in the Bible organized by the four hierarchies of demons in Ephesians 6:12 help you against the unseen attacks against your mind, family, and nation.

OTHER BOOKS IN THE BASIC BIBLE SERIES

Covenants of God Series

The *Covenants of God* collection of The *Basic Bible Series* is a comprehensive exploration of the sacred agreements that form the backbone of God's relationship with humanity, as revealed throughout Scripture.

TESTIMONIALS

If these prayers helped you in any way please visit:

www.basicbibleseries.com/contact

Use this as a way to publicly give glory to God!

Scan the QR Code to leave a testimonial!

Spirit Names Across Bible Translations

When looking up evil spirits in the Bible, they can be called many different names depending on the Bible translation you read. For purposes of this book, the Young's Literal Translation (YLT) is used initially to understand the exact name of the spirit from the original Hebrew or Greek texts. A different translation may be used when quoting scripture.

As you read through this prayer book, you may recall other spirits you have read about in the Bible and wonder why they were not included. Every effort was made to include every evil spirit mentioned, but it may just have a different name depending on the translation you read. The different spirit name translations are footnoted for each spirit across eight different popular Bible translations: KJV, YLT, NASB, NIV, NKJV, NLT, ESV, and CSB.

Contents

Demon Hierarchy

EPHESIANS 6:12

"For we do not wrestle against flesh and blood, but against principalities, against powers, against the rulers of the darkness of this age, against spiritual hosts of wickedness in the heavenly places." (Ephesians 6:12)

Demon Hierarchy

In this verse we see a hierarchy of four demon classes that war against us in this world. They operate in heavenly places that are unseen by us. They are the masters of the unseen because they can see what we cannot. This makes it an unfair fight for ordinary people, but as Christians we have the power of the Holy Spirit inside of us and authority given to us by Jesus over every demonic force.

This prayer book is broken up into the four areas of demonic attacks evident in our world today. They seek to tear down nations, draw us away from God's word through other religions, cripple our minds and bodies, and seek knowledge apart from God through occult practices. Spiritual warfare is real and it is all around us. You must be aware of these as the Bible states, *"My people are destroyed for lack of knowledge."* (Hosea 4:6) Time to get equipped.

Principalities

This elite group is not found doing Satan's dirty work among ordinary people. They are high-ranking demonic entities that are chief rulers in the spiritual realm. These beings oversee territories, nations, and societal structures:

> *"Say unto the king and to the queen, Humble yourselves, sit down: for your principalities shall come down, even the crown of your glory."*
> (Jeremiah 13:18, KJV)

Rather than engaging in direct temptations among ordinary people, they exert influence on earthly governments, leaders, and cultural strongholds. This hierarchy underscores that spiritual warfare extends beyond personal battles, impacting homes, communities, and nations as believers confront these forces opposing God's kingdom.

Powers

Evil powers are other religions that keep us from worshipping the one true God. God works in partnership with man to produce good in the earth. God has the power, we have the authority. In a fallen world, Satan works through our authority to establish other religions to keep our eye off God or pervert our understanding of God. This blinds unbelievers to the gospel:

> *"But even if our gospel is veiled, it is veiled to those who are perishing, whose minds the god of this age has blinded, who do not believe, lest the light of the gospel of the glory of Christ, who is the image of God, should shine on them."* (2 Corinthians 4:3-4)

When Jesus comes back, He is coming back for the body of the church to establish His eternal kingdom. The heavenly powers that produce false doctrines will be shaken:

> *"Immediately after the tribulation of those days the sun will be darkened, and the moon will not give its light; the stars will fall from heaven, and the powers of the heavens will be shaken."* (Matthew 24:29)

Rulers of the Darkness of this Age

Symbolically, darkness represents everything opposed to God and His ways. Spiritually, darkness describes a state of living in sin without knowledge or fellowship with God, often due to a hardened heart, rebellion, or Satan's influence blinding minds to the gospel.

Rulers of darkness are evil spirits that afflict us personally whether by tempting us into sin, deceiving us, or inhabiting us, causing physical or mental issues.

Spiritual Hosts of Wickedness in the Heavenly Places

The host of heaven appears frequently in the Old Testament often in contexts related to either celestial bodies (the stars, sun, or moon) or angelic beings. In creation contexts, it denotes stars. In divine council scenes, it refers to angels. In verses about idolatry, it clearly means celestial bodies worshiped as deities:

This group of demons influence occult practices and forbidden knowledge. The Bible refers to these practices as divination, fortune-telling, sorcery, magic, witchcraft, mediums, necromancy, omens, astrology, charmers, wizardry, enchantment and other occult practices. God forbids us to participate in any of these.

Armor of God

EPHESIANS 6:13-17

"Therefore put on the full armor of God, so that when the day of evil comes, you may be able to stand your ground, and after you have done everything, to stand. Stand firm then, with the belt of truth buckled around your waist, with the breastplate of righteousness in place, and with your feet fitted with the readiness that comes from the gospel of peace. In addition to all this, take up the shield of faith, with which you can extinguish all the flaming arrows of the evil one. Take the helmet of salvation and the sword of the Spirit, which is the word of God." (Ephesians 6:13-17, NIV)

Armor of God

We have six pieces of armor that God provides to use as weapons to combat the weapons of Satan. In putting this armor on and wielding the sword of the spirit, we are engaging in spiritual warfare against evil.

Belt of Truth

One of our major weapons against demonic forces is truth. If you want to defeat sin, pursue truth. If truth is our weapon, then Satan's weapon against us is lies and deception. If you believe lies, you will be held back from the purposes of God.

Breastplate of Righteousness

Notice it's a breastplate so it covers your heart. Righteousness by faith is armor against condemnation and sin. Satan ensnares us through the weaknesses of our flesh and living in sin. Unrepentant sin gives Satan place to steal, kill, and destroy.

Shoes of Gospel of Peace

Peace is a weapon against strife and division. Satan lies to us and makes us feel like God doesn't love us or he tries to get us to war with family and our neighbors. We defeat Satan by loving each other and receiving peace with God through the blood of the cross.

Shield of Faith

Satan tries to get us to doubt God and he wants to produce unbelief. We fight back by developing our faith and growing in it. Our faith will overcome anything if we learn to abide by it. However, even if our faith is strong, it's our doubt and unbelief that brings our shield down. Faith believes things we can't see.

Sometimes we put our physical circumstances and what we see and feel above our faith.

Helmet of Salvation

Helmets cover our head and protects our mind. We must constantly be renewing our mind to the Word of God instead of what others are doing or saying. God has already saved us, but the warfare that happens in our minds is where the battle is either lost or won.

Sword of the Spirit

God's word is a sword and a spiritual weapon against Satan. When the Word of God is put in our heart and spoken out of our mouth, it's like a sword that torments evil spirits. We can't use natural weapons against spiritual beings. Satan's weapon against us is any word other than the Word of God. God's word releases blessings in our lives. Anyone's word against you is a spiritual weapon of Satan and we have to counter that in prayer. This is why we have to pray for those who are against us because they don't realize the enemy is using them.

Principalities

GODS THAT INFLUENCE NATIONS

*"He worked in Christ when He raised Him from the dead and seated Him at His right hand in the heavenly places, **far above all principality and power and might and dominion**, and every name that is named, not only in this age but also in that which is to come. And He put all things under His feet, and gave Him to be head over all things to the church, which is His body, the fullness of Him who fills all in all."* (Ephesians 1:20-23)

Gods That Influence Nations

In the unseen spirit realm, a relentless war wages against principalities of our physical world. Demonic entities extend their influence far beyond individual souls, often establishing strongholds over entire nations, cultures, and societies. They are active forces that orchestrate chaos, deception, and bondage, seeking to undermine God's sovereignty and ensnare humanity in webs of sin and despair. As believers called to stand firm in prayer, we must first recognize their strategies, for ignorance is their greatest ally.

Through subtle infiltration and overt domination, these principalities labor to overcome us, eroding our faith, fracturing our societies, and diverting us from the path God intended. Consider how these principalities operate like shadowy overlords, assigning lesser spirits to execute their agendas on earth. They exploit human vulnerabilities to gain footholds that grow into fortresses.

The first god to get a foothold into a nation is Baal. He manifests as a principality of prosperity and materialism, tempting societies to worship wealth, power, and abundance over the true Provider, Jehovah Jireh. He separates biblical principles from public discourse, untangling church and state in an attempt to strip God's order from His ordained purpose for government. By promising provision apart from God, Baal sows seeds of greed and rebellion, dividing communities and nations using the influence of media and entertainment.

With the culture numbed, Ashtaroth amplifies sin through seduction, corrupting all morality. She injects sexuality into every sphere of the culture. She breaks all the rules and oversteps every boundary. Anything good is perverted and twisted to be the opposite. Debauchery, drugs, and drunkenness are used to alter states of mind. She is violent and promiscuous and attacks those who question her perversions.

Then Molech brings ultimate destruction to a society, the devaluation of life and demand of child sacrifice. He rules through spirits of death and destruction, manifesting in modern scourges like abortion and human trafficking. Ashtaroth's promiscuous ways provide an abundance of innocent souls who are offered as sacrifices on the altars of convenience and ideology. He is the destroyer of life, the greatest abomination, symbolizing the ultimate sign of a nation that has turned entirely against the ways of God.

The spirit of whoredom is what happens to a people when demonic principalities take hold. They collectively commit spiritual adultery against God, their husband. Yet, in the face of such formidable foes, we are not left defenseless. The beginning of victory lies in awareness and alignment with Christ's authority. He has disarmed principalities and powers, making a public spectacle of them through His triumph on the cross (Colossians 2:15). All of society is not lost when Christians take a stand for their nation through prayer. The authority given to us is the key to dismantling these strongholds over our nation. Arm yourself with the full armor of God and stand resolute in your faith, for the Sword of the Spirit is our greatest weapon in warfare against the enemy.

BAAL

*"Then the children of Israel did evil in the sight of the Lord, and served the **Baals**; and they forsook the Lord God of their fathers, who had brought them out of the land of Egypt; and they followed other gods from among the gods of the people who were all around them, and they bowed down to them."* (Judges 2:11-12)

Baal[1]

Baal was a prominent Canaanite deity associated with fertility, rain, storms, and agricultural prosperity. He was worshiped by surrounding pagan nations and represented the allure of material abundance by promising fruitfulness, increase, gain, and economic prosperity to those who honored him.

As the Israelites settled in the Promised Land and began farming, the practical temptations of Baal's promises drew many away from exclusive devotion to God. Instead of trusting God for provision, they invoked Baal through rituals and idolatry, viewing him as a more immediate source of blessing. This shift marked the embodiment of paganism for Israel. Baal became the substitute deity that people turned to when rejecting or drifting from the true God.

Scripture identifies Baal worship as a primary cause of Israel's spiritual apostasy and ultimate national destruction. The spirit or mission of Baal is to progressively estrange a nation that once knew God: first causing it to stop actively knowing Him, then to forget Him entirely, and finally to erase all memory that it ever knew Him. This led Israel to become completely alienated from the God of its foundation, resulting in moral decay and divine judgment.

Today, a nation that turns from God starts with removing prayer from public spaces. Then Baal's agenda permeates every sphere of the culture. Christian values stop being represented in newspapers, media, entertainment, and politics. The Ten Commandments are stripped from government institutions. With God's foundational laws out of public view, sin can be embraced and culture wars begin. When the Spirit of God is removed, we leave an empty house for other spirits to take possession (Matthew 12:43-45).

---

1. Baal (NLT)

Baalim (KJV, YLT)

Baals (NASB, NIV, NKJV, ESV, CSB)

Prosperity today is no longer measured by agriculture. Today prosperity is measured by wealth. The symbol of Baal in the times of Ancient Israel was represented as a calf or young bull,

> *"Aaron answered them, 'Take off the gold earrings that your wives, your sons and your daughters are wearing, and bring them to me.' He took what they handed him and made it into an idol cast in the shape of a **calf**. Then they said, 'These are your gods, Israel, who brought you up out of Egypt.'"* (Exodus 32:4, NIV)

Our modern Baal idol is the bull representing the stock market, or the bull market. The stock market is a symbol of wealth and a tool to become prosperous. There is nothing wrong with wealth in of itself, as it can be a blessing from God. The issue arises when we idolize money, material possessions, and gain above all else. The bull is a symbol of a nation falling away from God. Fortunately we can turn back and our best hope of doing so is through prayer.

Repentance From Idolatrous Prosperity

Heavenly Father,

We come before You in deep repentance for allowing prosperity to become idolatrous in our nation, turning Your blessing into an object of ultimate trust and priority above You. Wealth itself is not the sin, but the love of money, greed, and covetousness that elevate it above You transform it into idolatry. In times of abundance our hearts have grown proud, forgetting that every good gift comes from You.

Gracious God, we confess how many in our land chase material gain as their primary purpose. In our consumer-driven culture, we fear loss of prosperity more than displeasing You. Have mercy on us for allowing comfort and abundance to breed spiritual apathy, where we feel blessed by wealth yet grow lukewarm in wholehearted pursuit of Jesus.

Lord we repent of this national idolatry and ask You to awaken consciences across our country to recognize prosperity's dangers and return to You as our ultimate security. Strip away the pride that comes with plenty and revive a spirit of contentment that trusts You in scarcity or abundance. Turn our hearts from loving money to loving You. May this repentance bring renewal, freeing us from the bondage of material obsession and drawing our nation back to the One who is our true Provider and greatest treasure.

In Jesus' name we pray,

Amen.

Prayer for Revival in the Education System

Heavenly Father,

We come before You acknowledging that dark spiritual forces have long sought to ensnare our children, the future of our nation. These influences target the young aiming to pull them away from Your truth. We confess that the removal of prayer from our schools marked a pivotal turning point, opening the door for separation from Your presence in the place where minds are shaped and character is formed.

Lord God, we lift up our schools and ask You to expose and remove any teachers or influences that carry hidden agendas contrary to Your Word. Protect our children from teachings that twist truth, promote division, or lead them away from the purpose You intend for them. Raise up godly educators who will boldly reflect Your light in every lesson and interaction. Surround our young ones with Your hedge of protection, guarding their hearts and minds from the enemy's schemes that aim to alienate them from the future You have prepared.

Gracious Father, we ask for a fresh outpouring of Your Spirit upon every classroom and every child in our nation. Restore the transmission of genuine faith so that our nation might once again be rooted in Your truth. Let revival begin in the hearts of the young, drawing our entire country back into close fellowship with You.

In Jesus' name we pray,

Amen.

Prayer for Godly Influence in the News Media

Heavenly Father,

We come before You seeking Your divine intervention for a profound revival in the media and news outlets of our nation. We confess that much of the mainstream media has drifted into clear bias, often portraying Christianity in a negative light. Journalism has shifted from neutral, fact-based reporting to activist-driven narratives that seek to reshape society rather than fairly present all perspectives. Lord, we ask You to expose these imbalances and raise up voices that honor truth and integrity once more.

Gracious God, we lament how the relentless 24/7 news cycle bombards people with endless voices, sensational scandals, and divisive controversies. This constant flood erodes discernment, fosters complacency, and opens doors to deception and inaccuracy that undermine public trust. We pray You would restore honesty and accountability in reporting, protect viewers from manipulative content, and revive a commitment to balanced, truthful coverage.

Lord of all truth, we cry out for Your Spirit to move powerfully across every platform, studio, and screen in our nation. Awaken journalists, producers, and media leaders to their responsibility before You, turning many toward righteousness and away from agendas contrary to our faith. Heal the broken trust in news, draw our nation back to seeking truth in Your light, and use renewed media to glorify You and strengthen Your people.

In Jesus' name we pray,

Amen.

Prayer for Godly Influence in Entertainment

Heavenly Father,

We bow before You, asking for a powerful revival to touch the television and movie entertainment industry across our nation. So much of what is produced glorifies behaviors You clearly condemn. Graphic violence floods screens in desensitizing ways, harming minds and filling them with darkness rather than peace. Nudity, explicit scenes, crude innuendo, and the constant objectification of bodies have become commonplace, eroding purity and respect for the dignity You created in every person.

Gracious God, we lament the casual blasphemy and mockery directed at You, Jesus, and the Christian faith that appears in scripts and dialogue. Productions increasingly draw people into spiritual deception and away from Your light. These influences subtly, or not so subtly, undermine biblical teachings on marriage, identity, and family.

Lord, we ask for Your Spirit to move mightily through every studio, script, and screen across our nation. Let this revival awaken producers, writers, actors, and executives to use their talents for Your glory, creating entertainment that draws people closer to You. Break the grip of spiritual distraction and moral compromise, restore a hunger for wholesome and inspiring stories, and use renewed media to spark faith in the next generation. Heal what has been corrupted, redeem what has been lost, and let entertainment point toward Your truth and beauty.

In Jesus' name we pray,

Amen.

Prayer for Godly Influence in Music

Heavenly Father,

We come to You with concerned hearts, asking for a revival in the music of our nation. We recognize that words carry great power, but when united with music, they penetrate hearts swiftly and deeply, which is why singing Your praises together in church builds faith so effectively. Yet much of mainstream music today celebrates immorality, sexual promiscuity, lust, drug use, violence, greed, pride, and rebellion, often framing these as empowering, fun, or liberating choices.

Gracious God, we lament how popular music so frequently exalts the self above all, promoting personal fulfillment at any cost. It idolizes fame, wealth, beauty, fleeting relationships, and selfish desires. We ask You to expose these distortions, protect young ears and minds from their subtle poison, and inspire artists to produce music that reflects Your design for purity.

Lord of all harmony, we cry out for Your Spirit to sweep powerfully through studios, stages, and streaming platforms across our nation. Let this revival transform the industry, raising up songwriters, performers, and producers who use their gifts to glorify You. As music shapes worldviews on a massive scale, especially among the young, may renewed songs restore a generation's focus on You, drawing our nation back to praise that truly transforms hearts and cultures.

In Jesus' name we pray,

Amen.

Prayer for Fiscal Responsibility

Heavenly Father,

We come before You in repentance for our nation's reckless stewardship regarding the massive national debt that now burdens us so heavily. You entrust resources as provision to be managed wisely, yet we have pursued endless borrowing to fund today's consumption. This unsustainable path has shifted crushing burdens onto our children and grandchildren putting them in chains of future obligation. Lord, forgive us for this folly, and awaken our hearts to the gravity of treating Your gifts with such carelessness.

Gracious God, we confess how this mounting debt cripples the middle class and poor through inflation, reduced services, or economic strain. We repent of greed masked as necessity and of a spirit that trusts in human systems more than in Your provision. Have mercy on us, and turn our nation from this path of decline toward one of responsible management.

Lord of all provision, we pray for our leaders to embrace fiscal responsibility. Help each of us personally to model debt-free living where possible, practicing wise stewardship in our homes as a testimony to Your ways. Grant us the faith to trust Your ultimate security, while acting diligently to reduce burdens and restore soundness. May this repentance lead to renewal, freeing our nation from financial bondage and drawing us closer to You as our true Provider.

In Jesus' name we pray,

Amen.

ASHTAROTH

*"They provoked the Lord to anger. They abandoned the Lord and served the Baals and the **Ashtaroth**."* (Judges 2:12-13, ESV)

*"The people of Israel again did what was evil in the sight of the Lord and served the Baals and the **Ashtaroth**."* (Judges 10:6, ESV)

Ashtaroth[1]

In biblical accounts and Canaanite mythology, Ashtaroth was a prominent goddess, a symbol of divine feminine power. She is depicted as the consort or wife of Baal. She embodied fertility, love, sensuality, and war, and was worshiped through ritualized sexual acts and prostitution. She exhibits an intense dual nature of passionate eroticism and violent combativeness. Myths depict her transforming genders or blurring male and female distinctions. On one side she embodies female empowerment where females take on the roles of men. On the other side, she aims to feminize and emasculate men, making them subservient.[2]

Ashtaroth's emergence in a nation typically follows the influence of Baal. Baal represents the initial turning away from God toward prosperity and materialism. Once the people are separated from God, Ashtaroth steps in to amplify sin, ushering in widespread moral erosion. Over time, long-held ethical foundations and restraining moral values begin to overturn, giving way to sexual immorality and the rejection of divine boundaries of male and female. Thus, Ashtaroth accelerates a nation's progression into deeper paganism, further alienating it from the holiness and order established by God.

---

1. Ashtaroth (KJV, YLT, NASB, ESV)
   Ashtoreths (NIV, NKJV, NLT, CSB)

2. Ashtaroth manifested herself in different forms (Asherah, wooden poles, groves, cakes for the Queen of Heaven). She is mentioned many times throughout the Bible however it does not go into great detail on her influences. For the purposes of this book, her description is taken from texts about pagan mythologies.

Repentance From Sexual Immorality

Heavenly Father,

We come before You with heartfelt repentance for the widespread sexual immorality that has permeated our nation. We confess that we have turned away from Your good design for sexuality and instead embraced and celebrated behaviors that You call sin. Lord, we repent of the pride that justifies these choices and the complacency that tolerates them. Forgive us for allowing darkness to flourish while light has been dimmed.

Gracious God, we acknowledge how this immorality has brought devastating consequences to our nation. Our culture's glorification of sexual freedom has led many astray, especially the young, who are bombarded with messages that mock purity and redefine love apart from You. Have mercy on us, Father; cleanse us from this uncleanness. Break the strongholds of lust and deception. Restore a reverence for the sacredness of human sexuality as You intended it.

Lord, we cry out for a national revival of repentance. Awaken consciences across our nation to recognize sexual sin for what it is. Convict those who promote immorality, and raise up voices who proclaim Your better way. Heal the broken and pour out Your Spirit to renew minds and transform desires. May our nation once again honor sex only within the marriage covenant. We trust in Your forgiveness through the blood of Jesus and Your power to make all things new.

In Jesus' name we pray,

Amen.

Repentance for Our Cultural Celebration of Homosexuality

Heavenly Father,

We come before You in deep repentance for our nation's widespread celebration of homosexuality, which has permeated our culture and entertainment. It has been portrayed as normal through movies, shows, music, and public events. This injection of deceptive ideologies has confused minds, especially the young, and drawn many away from Your sacred design for human intimacy. Lord, forgive us for embracing and promoting what grieves Your heart, and we ask You to expose the lies that fuel this cultural shift.

Gracious God, we grieve profoundly for those who struggle with same-sex attraction, recognizing the pain, confusion, and isolation they often endure. We lift them up to You, asking for Your tender mercy to surround them. Reveal the root causes of their desires and grant them the strength to break those chains. Heal their hearts, Father, and provide godly support, helping them walk in the identity You created them for.

Lord of deliverance, we cry out for a supernatural turnaround in our nation, halting the glorification of homosexuality in every sphere. Awaken consciences to reject the normalization of this sin. May those bound by this stronghold experience true liberation in Christ, becoming testimonies of Your transforming grace, and may our nation reflect Your holiness once more.

In Jesus' name we pray,

Amen.

Repentance for Embracing Transgenderism

Heavenly Father,

We come before You in repentance for our nation's embrace and celebration of transgenderism. This cultural shift glorifies altering bodies that defy the beautiful distinctions You established, leading many into deception masked as self-expression and freedom. We grieve how this has become normalized, with ideologies that defy Your creation order. Lord, turn our nation from applauding what harms, expose the deception, and restore reverence for the bodies and identities You assigned.

Gracious God, we lift up every person who has fallen into the trap of transitioning their bodies. Surround those wrestling with gender dysphoria, influenced by societal pressures, or seeking relief from inner turmoil, with Your mercy. Heal their wounds that may have fueled this path, and grant them courage to pursue true identity in Christ rather than fleeting affirmations from the world. Protect them from further harm.

Lord, we cry out for a profound awakening across our nation to turn from celebrating transgenderism and return to honoring Your unchanging truth about gender and humanity. Expose the agendas that profit from confusion and exploitation and restore families fractured by this division. May those who have transitioned find supernatural reversal where possible, becoming testimonies of Your power to transform lives. Heal our land from this delusion, revive a reverence for Your creation, and let Your light dispel the darkness that has gripped so many.

In Jesus' name we pray,

Amen.

Prayer Against Demasculinating Men

Heavenly Father,

We come before You in urgent prayer, confessing that our nation has allowed spiritual deception to undermine the God-given design of manhood. You created men in Your image with qualities meant to protect, provide, and guide. Yet today, many voices in our culture promote a weakening of these traits, portraying masculinity as outdated or harmful. Lord, we grieve over this demasculinization that strips men from the roles You ordained.

Gracious God, we ask You to intervene powerfully against every influence that seeks to erode manhood. Restore in men a holy boldness to reject apathy. Break the chains of fear, confusion, and cultural pressure that cause men to shrink back from godly authority. Awaken boys and men to the joy of using their God-given strength to serve, protect, and disciple others. Expose the lies of toxic masculinity and replace them with Your vision of manhood.

Lord, we cry out for a revival of manhood across our nation. Raise up fathers who lead their families, men who stand as protectors against evil, and leaders in the work place. Heal the wounds caused by absent fathers, distorted role models, and societal shifts that leave generations adrift. Pour out Your Spirit to empower men to reclaim their calling. Turn our nation back to honoring Your design for manhood, that men might rise and fulfill their purpose for Your glory.

In Jesus' name we pray,

Amen.

Prayer Exposing the Destruction of Feminism

Heavenly Father,

We come before You with hearts burdened for the women of our nation who have been influenced by feminism's challenge to traditional gender norms. This has lead to the rejection of the beautiful roles You designed for harmony between men and women. As believers, we already affirm the equal value and dignity of women, rejecting any idea of inherent superiority between genders. Yet feminism has sown confusion by suggesting fulfillment comes from dismantling these norms rather than turning to You for true purpose and contentment.

Gracious God, we pray that women would recognize the destructive devaluation of motherhood and homemaking promoted by feminism, which portrays these callings as lesser or oppressive compared to careers and independence. Help them see that true fulfillment blooms from embracing the nurturing, life-giving roles You honor. Stir their spirits to turn from these misleading ideas, discovering the profound satisfaction that comes from living in obedience to Your design.

Lord, we pray that women across our nation would recognize how these feminist ideals have contributed to growing unhappiness and a progressive decline in well-being. Heal the wounds inflicted by unfulfilled promises of empowerment. Raise up voices of courage to counter these destructive narratives, and let a wave of repentance lead to renewal where women flourish in Your grace. May our nation turn from these deceptions and honor Your beautiful design for womanhood.

In Jesus' name we pray,

Amen.

Prayer Against Violent Protests

Heavenly Father,

We come before You in grief, pleading for You to bring an end to the violent protests that have erupted across our nation in recent times. These demonstrations have too frequently escalated into chaos causing clashes with law enforcement, property destruction, assaults, and threats that endanger lives and tear communities apart. Lord, we repent of the hatred, pride, and unwillingness to listen that allow such violence to take root, and we ask You to restrain every hand raised in harm.

Gracious God, we acknowledge that these outbreaks reflect deeper wounds in our society that dehumanize opponents. This unrest not only disrupts peace but also distracts from addressing root issues with truth. We pray for Your supernatural intervention to diffuse tensions, expose agitators who incite destruction, and inspire leaders at every level to pursue accountability.

Lord, we cry out for Your Spirit to move powerfully over our land, convicting hearts of the futility and sin of violence. Raise up peacemakers among citizens and believers who will model humility and love even toward those who they disagree with. Heal the fractures that fuel these protests. Restore order and guide our nation toward unity rather than division and strife. May Your justice prevail, Your mercy abound, and violent unrest cease as people turn to You for true hope and change.

In Jesus' name we pray,

Amen.

Prayer to Address the Drug Crisis in Our Nation

Heavenly Father,

We come before Your throne proclaiming a mighty turnaround for our nation from the devastating grip of drug abuse. For too long, addiction to drugs has enslaved millions. We declare that this bondage is not unbreakable, for You are the God who sets captives free and breaks every chain. Lord, we proclaim today that the tide is turning. Your power is greater than any chemical stronghold, and we stand in agreement that the era of drugs dominating our nation is coming to an end.

Gracious God, we lift up every person trapped in addiction. Pour out Your Holy Spirit to those affected in our nation with supernatural strength to say no to temptation. Raise up armies of intercessors, godly counselors, transformed former addicts, and bold ministries to walk alongside the broken. We proclaim healing for bodies ravaged by withdrawal and long-term damage. Restore families that have been torn apart.

Lord, we declare that this nation will no longer be defined by drugs but by a sweeping revival of sobriety and purpose in You. Turn mourning into dancing, ashes into beauty, and hopelessness into hope as thousands upon thousands experience deliverance and step into a new life. Let testimonies of freedom multiply, drawing others to the Light. We proclaim turnaround now and give You glory for the breakthrough that is coming.

In Jesus' name we pray,

Amen.

MOLECH

*"And they built the high places of Baal which are in the Valley of the Son of Hinnom, to cause their sons and their daughters to pass through the fire to **Molech**, which I did not command them, nor did it come into My mind that they should do this abomination."* (Jeremiah 32:35)

Molech[1]

In the Bible, Molech was a detestable Canaanite deity associated with the most horrific form of idolatry: the sacrifice of children. Worshipers offered their own sons and daughters as burnt sacrifices to him, passing them through fire in rituals. The Bible speaks of this act as the most abominable.

Molech represents the ultimate progression and darkest endpoint of a nation's turning away from God. Following the influence of Baal and Ashtaroth, Molech emerges as the spirit that demands the shedding of innocent blood. Particularly, the sacrifice of children by their parents, or in our modern world: abortion.

This manifests in the devaluation of human life to its lowest point, where a culture embraces cold, inhuman destruction under the guise of convenience, rights, or necessity. The unwanted fruits of sexual promiscuity influenced by Ashtaroth are offered on Molech's altar, marking a society that has fully inverted God's order: instead of protecting the innocent and valuing life as sacred, it sanctions and normalizes their destruction.

---

1. Molech (YLT, KJV, NASB, NKJV, NLT, ESV, CSB)
   Molek (NIV)

Prayer to End Abortion

Heavenly Father,

We come before You in humble repentance and earnest plea. Your holy word reveals that life is sacred from its very beginning, a precious gift bestowed by Your hand even in the womb. The unborn child is fully human, fashioned in Your image with purpose and dignity from the moment of conception. We confess that our nation has strayed far from this truth, and we ask You to awaken hearts to the divine sanctity of every life You form.

Lord, we lament how the widespread acceptance of abortion reflects a deeper rebellion against Your perfect design for life. This practice has dulled our conscience, normalizing the ending of vulnerable lives and weakening the sacred duty to defend the innocent. It has wounded countless women with deep emotional scars that linger long after the act. We pray earnestly that You would heal these broken hearts and turn our society away from this path of destruction.

Gracious God, we see the heavy toll this has taken on our nation. These choices have deepened divisions, pitting "choice" against "life" in ways that harden hearts and obstruct the unity You command among Your people. We beseech You to intervene with Your mighty power and bring an end to abortion in our land. Restore us to Your ways, that we may once again honor life as the gift it truly is.

In Jesus' name we pray,

Amen.

Prayer to Restore Parental Instincts

Heavenly Father,

We come before You on behalf of men and women who face the news of a child conceived outside of marriage. You design life intentionally, knitting each little one together in the womb. In these moments of fear, awaken within their hearts the natural instincts You have placed there. The deep, God-given maternal urge to nurture and bond with the child growing within. The strong paternal drive to protect their offspring at all costs. Restore these holy impulses that sin and fear have dulled, so they may see this child not as a burden but as a precious being entrusted by You.

Lord, we ask You to stir their souls with the protective love You intend for parents. Remind them that even in difficult circumstances, Your grace is sufficient to empower them to choose life and embrace the calling to raise this child. Heal any wounds that threaten to override these instincts, and replace them with courage to safeguard the life You have created. Let Your Spirit move powerfully to draw them toward the path of nurturing and protection.

Gracious God, we pray that these parents respond to Your awakening call. That they would experience Your forgiveness and support. Surround them with Your peace and guide them step by step to honor the life You have given. May their decision to embrace parenthood reflect Your heart for the defenseless and bring glory to Your name.

In Jesus' name we pray,

Amen.

Prayer to End Trafficking

Heavenly Father,

We come before You in anguish, crying out for Your mighty intervention to end the horrific trafficking of children and others that plagues our nation and the world. This evil trade has ensnared countless innocents, with millions suffering globally in modern slavery. Children, often the most defenseless, are targeted for their youth and innocence, torn from safety, manipulated, and commodified by those driven by greed and darkness. Lord, we grieve deeply over every life stolen, every future shattered, and every family broken by this abomination.

Gracious God, we lift up every victim who endures unimaginable suffering. Surround them with Your supernatural protection, expose their captors, and loose Your delivering power to set them free. Heal their deep wounds and restore what has been stolen through Your redeeming love. Raise up rescuers, law enforcement, and ministries to dismantle these criminal networks, and provide comprehensive care for survivors.

Lord, we proclaim by faith that this darkness will not prevail. Break the strongholds of traffickers. Stir leaders, communities, and Your church to act decisively in prevention, rescue, and restoration of the victims. May trafficked children and others find freedom, families be reunited, and our land repent of allowing such evil to persist. We trust in Your power to bring justice rolling like waters and righteousness like an ever-flowing stream.

In Jesus' name we pray,

Amen.

SPIRIT OF WHOREDOM

*"My people inquire of a piece of wood, and their walking staff gives them oracles. For a **spirit of whoredom** has led them astray, and they have left their God to play the whore."* (Hosea 4:12, ESV)

*"Their deeds do not permit them to return to their God. For the **spirit of whoredom** is within them, and they know not the Lord."* (Hosea 5:4, ESV)

Spirit of Whoredom[1]

The spirit of whoredom represents a profound and pervasive inclination toward spiritual unfaithfulness. It is a betrayal of the exclusive covenant relationship with the Lord. This spirit manifests in Israel's repeated idolatry, akin to adultery in a sacred marriage. The prophet Hosea's own union with an unfaithful wife serves as a parable of God's heartache over His people's wanderings.

Having examined the influences of Baal, Ashtaroth, and Molech we see how they collectively fuel this spirit. Baal entices with promises of prosperity and power, Ashtaroth seduces through sensuality and debauchery, and Molech demands the ultimate sacrifice of innocence, all drawing hearts away from the one true God. Together, they form a dark parody of the Holy Trinity, orchestrated by Satan to pervert divine truth and lead civilizations into moral decay and rebellion.

The spirit of whoredom leads the people astray, prompting them to seek guidance from lifeless idols—be they golden calves, Asherah poles, or the altars of sacrifice to these false gods—rather than the living Lord. It takes root deep within, rendering genuine repentance elusive, as habitual sin hardens the heart and obscures intimate knowledge of God.

In Hosea's overarching prophecy, this spirit underscores Israel's intractable defiance: their idolatry was not mere lapses but an entrenched disposition, one that barred any authentic return to God without His merciful intervention. Yet, the book resounds with hope, revealing God's jealous love and His pledge of eventual restoration, even amid such profound betrayal.

---

1. Spirit of Harlotry (NKJV)

Spirit of Infidelity (NASB)

Spirit of Promiscuity (CSB)

Spirit of Prostitution (NIV, NLT - played the prostitute, doesn't say spirit)

Spirit of Whoredom (KJV, YLT, ESV)

In our own era, this spirit persists, subtly eroding nations once anchored in biblical foundations through cultural shifts and spiritual compromise. Demonic principalities, wielding influences like those of Baal, Ashtaroth, and Molech, sway governments and societies, turning them into faithless spouses who forsake their divine Husband for fleeting idols. The biblical warning echoes: unchecked disobedience and false worship invite judgment and downfall. Thus, it is vital to intercede in prayer for our nation. We must beseech God to expose these deceptions, break the hold of this spirit, and draw hearts back to faithful devotion.

Prayer for Our Elected Leaders in Government

Heavenly Father,

We come before You recognizing that all authority in government comes from Your divine appointment, and we lift up our elected leaders to You in prayer. Guide them to fulfill their roles with integrity and a sense of responsibility that honors Your sovereignty over all earthly powers. May they seek wisdom from You as they make decisions that affect the lives of many, aligning their actions with biblical principles.

Lord, we ask that You take hold of the hearts of our president, senators, representatives, and local officials, directing their thoughts and inclinations toward what is good and right. Surround them with wise counselors who point them toward decisions that uphold dignity and freedom for every citizen. Help them to resist influences that lead astray, instead channeling their efforts into paths that reflect Your righteous ways.

In Your mercy, continue to shape the course of our nation through these servants, ensuring that their leadership brings about stability and hope for future generations. Strengthen their resolve to act justly in times of challenge, and let Your peace guard their minds amid the pressures of office. We trust in Your ultimate plan, praying that through them, Your kingdom's values would shine brightly in our land.

In Jesus' name we pray,

Amen.

Prayer to Raise Up Christian Leaders

Heavenly Father,

We humbly come before You, asking that You would raise up a new generation of Christian men and women who are deeply rooted in faith, and committed to serving with integrity. Stir the hearts of young believers across our nation to pursue roles in federal, state, and local offices, as well as on school boards, where they can faithfully represent Your truth and values.

Prepare their hearts now so they grow into leaders who prioritize biblical principles in every decision they make. Prepare them through education, character development, and spiritual growth so that when the time comes, they step forward with courage and conviction. Grant them a deep understanding of Your principles so that every decision they make reflects justice, mercy, and righteousness for the good of all people.

We also ask Your blessing upon the parents, families, and churches raising up this next generation. Strengthen these homes with wisdom, patience, and unwavering commitment to instill biblical values from an early age. Provide the resources, protection, and grace needed for mothers and fathers to nurture children who love You deeply and desire to serve You faithfully in every sphere of life. May these families be filled with Your peace and joy as they partner with You in preparing servants who will one day lead with Christ-like character.

In Jesus' name we pray,

Amen.

Prayer for Unity in Our Nation

Heavenly Father,

We approach Your throne with humble hearts, acknowledging the divisions that have torn at the fabric of our nation and seeking Your mercy for our shared failings. We confess the ways in which pride, selfishness, and strife have driven wedges between us, pleading for Your forgiveness to wash over our land and mend what is broken. Restore us as a people united under Your guidance, turning our collective gaze toward reconciliation and shared purpose.

Lord, we pray for security and tranquility to envelop our nation, guarding against forces that seek to sow chaos and separation. Heal the wounds of discord that plague our communities, replacing bitterness with understanding and fostering bonds that reflect Your harmonious design. Draw us closer as one body, free from the chains of division, so that peace may flow through our streets and homes.

In Your infinite wisdom, unite us in a profound oneness that mirrors the depth of Your own relational essence, bridging differences and strengthening our resolve against fragmentation. May this revival of spirit lead to lasting healing, where forgiveness reigns and collective strength emerges from our renewed commitment. We entrust our nation's future to You, believing in Your power to transform division into enduring solidarity.

In Jesus' name we pray,

Amen.

Prayer to Strengthen the Family Unit

Heavenly Father,

We come before You with humble hearts, acknowledging that our society has drifted far from the ideal of strong, unified families. In our culture today, broken homes have become far too common, with many children growing up without the steady presence and guidance of both a loving father and mother in the same household. We see the consequences as the foundational building block of stable families erodes, leaving voids that are filled by the world's ways.

Lord, we pray for a renewal of the family unit, where children are raised in homes anchored by committed mothers and fathers. Restore the vision of families as the primary place where biblical values are nurtured, creating a virtuous cycle of stability that flourishes for generations. Help us as a people to honor and protect this sacred structure, so that future children may thrive contributing to a healthier, more resilient society.

We lift up single mothers and single fathers who carry heavy burdens alone. Grant them extraordinary strength, wisdom, and provision for their daily needs. Comfort them in their weariness, heal any wounds of loss or hardship, and bless their efforts to raise their children with love and purpose, even as we ask You to guide many toward restored or new family wholeness where possible.

In Jesus' name we pray,

Amen.

Prayer for Laws to Be Established by Godly Standards

Heavenly Father,

We come before You in humble repentance, recognizing that our nation's laws have often drifted from the moral standards rooted in the Judeo-Christian principles that once guided our foundations. We recognize laws grounded in godly wisdom provide a firm, unchanging framework that transcends fleeting human opinions, shifting cultural trends, or the whims of those in power, ensuring justice remains impartial and rights are truly secure for every person.

Lord, we thank You for the wisdom of our Founding Fathers, who acknowledged You as Creator and declared that essential rights are endowed by You, not granted by governments or majorities. Restore to our laws this sacred foundation, so they promote true equality and guide society with moral clarity. Renew in our leaders and citizens a deep reverence for Your eternal standards, and guard against the chaos and tyranny that overtake nations abandoning biblical morals.

Gracious God, we pray for a spiritual awakening in our land. May lawmakers, judges, and all who shape our statutes seek Your guidance to align human laws with divine justice. Protect us from perils that erode trust and invite oppression. Strengthen our commitment to honor You in public life, that our nation may stand as a beacon of ordered liberty rooted in godly truth.

In Jesus' name we pray,

Amen.

Prayer for National Awakening

Heavenly Father,

We come before You with contrite hearts, pleading for a great spiritual awakening to sweep across our nation. In a time when many have drifted from You, we ask that You stir the souls of men, women, and children to return to church with renewed hunger for Your presence. Ignite a deep desire within them to grow in faith, so that hearts once hardened may soften and lives once aimless may find purpose in You.

Lord, we pray that prayer would once again be welcomed and practiced openly in public places such as schools, courthouses, workplaces, and gatherings, without fear. Restore a reverence for Your name in the public square, that people would boldly acknowledge You as the source of all blessing and wisdom. May this revival of prayer foster unity and moral courage among our citizens, turning our nation back to the godly foundations that have sustained us from the start.

Gracious God, kindle in every heart a renewed and healthy pride in our great nation, rooted in gratitude for the freedoms and opportunities You have granted us. Help us to steward our nation with responsibility, and to stand together as one people under Your sovereign hand. Pour out Your Spirit upon us afresh, that this awakening would bear lasting fruit that honors You once more.

In Jesus' name we pray,

Amen.

Powers

DOCTRINAL DECEPTION

*"The manifold wisdom of God might be **made known by the church to the principalities and powers in the heavenly places**, according to the eternal purpose which He accomplished in Christ Jesus our Lord, in whom we have boldness and access with confidence through faith in Him. Therefore I ask that you do not lose heart at my tribulations for you, which is your glory."* (Ephesians 3:10-13)

Doctrinal Deception

In the shadowed corridors of the spiritual realm, where powers of darkness conspire against the light of truth, believers face an insidious battle against the subtle manipulations of doctrinal deception. These demonic powers weave their influence through counterfeit faiths and philosophies, drawing souls away from the gospel of Christ and into the snares of error and idolatry. As the Apostle Paul warned,

> *"For such are false apostles, deceitful workers, transforming themselves into apostles of Christ. And no wonder! For Satan himself transforms himself into an angel of light."* (2 Corinthians 11:13-14)

It is through this guise of enlightenment and tolerance that these powers seek to overcome us, promoting other religions as pathways to peace while subtly eroding the foundation of faith in the one true God.

At the heart of this deception lie spirits specifically empowered to distort doctrine and seduce the unwary. The spirit of antichrist denies the lordship of Jesus Christ, infiltrating belief systems that acknowledge a higher power but reject His incarnation and resurrection, manifesting in religions that portray Him as merely a prophet, teacher, or enlightened being rather than the Son of God. This spirit convinces multitudes that all paths lead to the divine, thus nullifying the exclusive claim of Christ:

> *"I am the way, the truth, and the life. No one comes to the Father except through Me."* (John 14:6)

Complementing this is the spirit of error, which sows confusion through twisted interpretations and half-truths, often embedded in ancient or modern spiritualities that blend elements of mysticism, humanism, or legalism, leading adherents to rely on works, rituals, or inner experiences over the grace of God.

Further amplifying the assault is the seducing spirit that lures through,

"doctrines of demons," (1 Timothy 4:1)

enticing people with promises of hidden knowledge, personal empowerment, or universal harmony found outside biblical revelation. This spirit operates prolifically in other religions, such as those rooted in New Age ideologies, that emphasize self-deification, reincarnation, or cosmic energies. The spirit aims to pull individuals away from the worship of God by offering counterfeit spiritual highs. These powers exploit human curiosity, using cultural syncretism to merge incompatible beliefs. This is seen in the rise of hybrid spiritual practices that dilute Christianity with eastern philosophies or occult elements, fostering apostasy and spiritual bondage under the banner of "enlightenment" or "inclusivity."

Yet, amid this pervasive deception, we stand equipped with the discerning power of the Holy Spirit and the unchanging Word of God, which exposes every lie and empowers us to resist. We will uncover targeted prayers to bind these deceptive powers, and strategies to reclaim ground lost to false religions. Let us begin by arming ourselves with the belt of truth, for in exposing the tactics of these powers, we pave the way for deliverance and revival.

SPIRIT OF ANTICHRIST

*"Beloved, do not believe every spirit, but test the spirits, whether they are of God; because many false prophets have gone out into the world. By this you know the Spirit of God: Every spirit that confesses that Jesus Christ has come in the flesh is of God, and every spirit that does not confess that Jesus Christ has come in the flesh is not of God. And this is the **spirit of the Antichrist**, which you have heard was coming, and is now already in the world."* (1 John 4:1-3)

Spirit of Antichrist[1]

The spirit of antichrist refers to a false spiritual influence or deceptive teaching that opposes the true identity of Jesus Christ. It is not primarily about a single future person (though it connects to the ultimate Antichrist figure), but a mindset or force that was already active in the world when John wrote his letter.

"Beloved, do not believe every spirit, but test the spirits, whether they are of God; because many false prophets have gone out into the world."

In the first verse, the apostle John instructs believers to test the spirits because many false prophets had gone out into the world. John uses *"spirits"* to refer to spiritual influences or teachings behind the people who claim to speak for God. The command is clear: Do not believe everything you hear. Instead, test these spirits to see if they are from God. Why? Because false prophets (people spreading deceptive teachings) were already active in the world. John is addressing a real, present danger in the church.

"By this you know the Spirit of God: Every spirit that confesses that Jesus Christ has come in the flesh is of God,"

In the second verse, John provides a simple, objective test: Does the teaching or influence confess that Jesus Christ has come in the flesh? *"Come in the flesh"* means Jesus is fully God who truly became fully human. He was not just a spirit or divine being who only appeared human. This confession is the hallmark of the *"Spirit of God."* Any teaching that affirms the true humanity and divinity of Jesus aligns with God's truth.

---

1. Spirit of Antichrist (KJV, YLT, NASB, NIV, NKJV, NLT, ESV, CSB)

In the third verse, the opposite is true: Any spirit that does not confess Jesus as having come in the flesh is not from God. John calls this *"the spirit of the antichrist"*, a deceptive, anti-Christ force that opposes the true identity of Jesus. He notes that believers had heard this antichrist was coming (likely referring to end-times prophecy), but it was already active in their time through false teachers.

This passage still applies: Any teaching or influence that denies Jesus' full humanity, full divinity, or the reality of His incarnation is not from God. It calls believers to be vigilant, grounded in the truth of Scripture, and confident in the Holy Spirit's guidance. 1 John 4:1-3 is a clear instruction on how to discern true from false teaching: The Spirit of God always confesses that Jesus Christ came in the flesh, while the spirit of the antichrist denies or distorts this truth.

Prayer to Expose Churches That Spread False Doctrine

Heavenly Father,

We come before You acknowledging that many churches in our nation have strayed from Your truth. They preach false doctrines disguised as Christianity that twist Your Word and lead souls astray. These teachings all claim to represent You. Lord, forgive us for complacency that has allowed wolves in sheep's clothing to infiltrate pulpits and deceive the faithful. We grieve over the confusion sown among believers and seekers alike, and we plead for Your light to pierce this darkness.

Gracious God, we pray that You would supernaturally expose these false teachers and their doctrines. Protect the vulnerable sheep from being misled and grant discernment to congregations to test every spirit. Remove the veils of deception that blind eyes and ears so that compromise might be laid bare before all. Have mercy on those who have been ensnared, drawing them back to the pure milk of Your Word.

Lord, we cry out for a mighty revival in our nation's churches, where false doctrines crumble under the weight of Your righteousness. Raise up faithful shepherds who proclaim the full counsel of Your Gospel, equipping believers to stand firm against deception. May this exposure purify Your bride, unite the body in sound doctrine, and draw a wandering nation back to genuine worship of You. Let Your kingdom come and Your will be done in every sanctuary across this land.

In Jesus' name we pray,

Amen.

Prayer Against False Religions in Our Land

Heavenly Father,

You have blessed our nation with the gift of freedom and prosperity. Our benevolent kindness has allowed our doors to be open for people from other walks of life and diverse beliefs to want to experience these gifts as well. We thank You for this liberty that reflects Your grace, yet we ask for Your guidance to preserve the foundational fabric of our society rooted in Christian values. Help us stand firm so that differing religious practices do not erode the principles that have shaped our communities and upheld our shared moral compass.

Lord, we lift up those among us who follow other paths and do not yet know You as Savior. Open their eyes and hearts to the truth of Your love, drawing them away from false gods that cannot save. May Your Holy Spirit move powerfully in their lives, leading them to repentance and faith in You alone, so that they too might experience the forgiveness and eternal life You freely offer.

Gracious God, protect Your faithful children from the temptations of exploring or adopting these foreign faiths. Strengthen our resolve to remain steadfast in our devotion to You, shielding our families and communities from influences that might dilute our commitment to Christianity. May we always prioritize Your teachings, fostering a generation that honors You above all else.

In Jesus' name we pray,

Amen.

Prayer for Those Who Rebel Against God

Heavenly Father,

We come before You with burdened hearts, interceding for those in our nation who actively rebel against You. Many have hardened their hearts through the allure of worldly pleasures that deliver only emptiness and separation from You. They mock Your name, dismiss Your Word, and live as though You do not see or care. Yet deep beneath their rebellion often lies hidden hurt. Lord, we lift them up to You, knowing that no one is beyond Your reach and that Your mercy pursues even the most defiant.

Gracious God, we ask You to break through the walls they have built. Awaken consciences that have grown numb to sin. Confront them in ways only You can. Draw near to those who feel too far gone, reminding them that Your arms remain open. Replace rebellion with repentance, defiance with surrender, and self-rule with joyful submission to the One who made them and knows them best.

Lord, we cry out for a mighty turning of hearts across this land. Let prodigals come to their senses, runaways return home, and hardened skeptics encounter the reality of Your living presence. Raise up testimonies of transformed rebels who once fought against You but now proclaim Your goodness. We trust in Your sovereign grace to do what no human effort can accomplish.

In Jesus' name we pray,

Amen.

Prayer for Boldness in Witnessing

Heavenly Father,

We come before You asking for a fresh outpouring of boldness upon every Christian in our nation to witness the Gospel to those around them. Too many of us have allowed fear of rejection, cultural pressure, or personal discomfort to silence our voices, even though You have called us to be salt and light in a darkening world. Stir our hearts with holy courage, remove every spirit of timidity, and fill us with the confidence that comes from knowing the power of the Gospel to save and transform lives.

Gracious God, open doors of opportunity for believers to share the hope found in Christ, and grant us wisdom to discern the right moments, words, and hearts that are ready to receive. Help us to live lives that make the Gospel attractive before we even speak a word. Raise up a generation of Christians who refuse to hide their faith and instead step forward in obedience and love.

Lord, we cry out for this boldness to ignite a massive wave of evangelism across our nation, drawing countless souls into Your kingdom and sparking a national revival. Let our witness be powerful, so that those who hear will see Jesus in us and be drawn to Him. To You be all the glory as Your people rise up and fulfill the Great Commission in our day.

In Jesus' name we pray,

Amen.

Spirit of Error

*"You are of God, little children, and have overcome them, because He who is in you is greater than he who is in the world. They are of the world. Therefore they speak as of the world, and the world hears them. We are of God. He who knows God hears us; he who is not of God does not hear us. By this we know the spirit of truth and the **spirit of error**."* (1 John 4:4-6)

Spirit of Error[1]

In the Bible, John contrasts the *"spirit of error"* with the *"spirit of truth."* This passage comes directly after the spirit of antichrist where John addresses the need for believers to *"test the spirits"* (1 John 4:1) to distinguish between true and false teachings or influences. The spirit of error refers to deceptive spiritual forces, false prophets, or doctrines that originate from the world (or Satan) rather than from God. These lead people astray by promoting ideas that contradict the core truths of Christianity.

> *"You are of God, little children, and have overcome them, because*
> *He who is in you is greater than he who is in the world."*

John addresses his readers affectionately as *"little children,"* affirming their identity as belonging to God. Believers have already *"overcome"* false teachers or deceptive spirits through faith in Christ. The key encouragement: The Holy Spirit (*"He who is in you"*) dwelling in Christians is more powerful than Satan (*"he who is in the world"*). This reassures believers of victory in spiritual battles.

> *"They are of the world. Therefore they speak as of the world, and*
> *the world hears them."*

"They" points to the false prophets or teachers who are aligned with worldly values and influences, not God. Their messages reflect secular, ungodly perspectives, and thus resonate with those who are also *"of the world"* (non-believers or those

---

1. Spirit of Deception (NLT, CSB)
   Spirit of Error (KJV, YLT, NASB, NKJV, ESV)
   Spirit of Falsehood (NIV)

opposed to God's truth). This highlights why false teachings can gain popularity; they appeal to human nature without the transformative power of the Gospel.

> *"We are of God. He who knows God hears us; he who is not of God does not hear us. By this we know the spirit of truth and the **spirit of error**."*

"We" refers to John and the apostles, whose teachings come directly from God. A test of authenticity: True believers (*"he who knows God"*) will recognize and accept apostolic doctrine, while those not aligned with God will reject it. This distinction reveals the *"spirit of truth"* (the Holy Spirit guiding genuine faith) versus the *"spirit of error"* (deceptive influences leading to falsehoods). It's a practical way to evaluate spiritual claims against Scripture.

Prayer for Others Who Practice New Age Thought

Heavenly Father,

We come before You for those in our nation who have been ensnared by New Age thoughts and practices that subtly draw them away from the truth of Christianity. These ideas have captivated many seeking peace, purpose, or power apart from You. Lord, we repent on their behalf for embracing deceptions that elevate human wisdom over Your divine revelation. We ask You to expose the emptiness and dangers hidden within these paths that lead souls astray from the Gospel.

Gracious God, we pray for a supernatural awakening among those entangled in New Age beliefs. Surround them with Your convicting presence, using circumstances, faithful witnesses, or inner unrest to reveal how these practices open doors to spiritual confusion. Grant them clarity to see that ultimate truth comes only through Jesus. Protect the vulnerable, especially the young, from being further drawn in by cultural trends that masquerade as harmless exploration.

Lord, we cry out for deliverance for every person caught in this web that subtly replaces you. Draw them away from these impersonal notions that promise self-directed enlightenment toward the abundant life found only through Jesus Christ. May Your Holy Spirit move in their heart, stirring conviction, granting clarity, and leading them to a personal encounter with You that brings lasting peace and wholeness in their life.

In Jesus' name we pray,

Amen.

Prayer to Expose the Folly of "Giving it Up to the Universe"

Heavenly Father,

We come to You for those in our nation who have turned to the universe as a source of power and guidance rather than to You. Many believe that by releasing things to the cosmos or trusting in its energy, they can manifest outcomes or find peace, yet this draws them away from the true love only You provide. Lord, open their eyes to the emptiness of these beliefs, back to You who spoke it into existence.

Gracious God, we pray for those ensnared by the idea that the universe wields ultimate power while ignoring Your omnipotent will and perfect plan. This deception replaces dependence on You with vague cosmic trust. Have mercy on them, Father; reveal Yourself through undeniable encounters, showing that true provision, and direction come from surrendering to You rather than impersonal energies. Awaken their spirits to recognize the difference between fleeting universal forces and Your eternal, unchanging might.

Lord, we cry out for a profound turning in hearts across our nation, drawing those who give things up to the universe back to You. Let them experience the freedom of casting cares upon You who cares for them personally. Raise up testimonies of transformed lives that glorify You, and use believers to gently point the way to the One who is infinitely more powerful and loving.

In Jesus' name we pray,

Amen.

Prayer For Those Who Are "Spiritual But Not Religious"

Heavenly Father,

We come before You for those in our nation who claim to be "spiritual but not religious", seeking meaning through personal experiences, nature, or vague energies while distancing themselves from faith in You. Many have turned away from Christianity due to past hurts or skepticism leaving them wandering without the anchor of Your truth. Lord, soften their hearts to recognize that true spirituality flows from a personal relationship with You, rather than isolated practices that cannot fully satisfy the soul.

Gracious God, we pray for an awakening among these drifters, revealing the emptiness of spirituality without surrender to the redemptive work of Christ. Help them see how rejecting Christianity in favor of individualism can mask a deeper rebellion against Your authority. Surround them with gentle encounters of Your presence that draw them beyond superficial spirituality toward genuine faith in You.

Lord, we cry out for these individuals to turn fully to You, repenting of self-reliant paths and embracing the richness of knowing You as Lord and Savior. Ignite in them a hunger for Your Word, fellowship with Your people, and the transformative power of the Gospel which You make alive through Your Spirit. May this turning lead to renewed lives, healed wounds, and a nation drawn closer to You in authentic worship.

In Jesus' name we pray,

Amen.

SEDUCING SPIRIT

*"Now the Spirit speaketh expressly, that in the latter times some shall depart from the faith, giving heed to **seducing spirits**, and doctrines of devils; Speaking lies in hypocrisy; having their conscience seared with a hot iron; Forbidding to marry, and commanding to abstain from meats, which God hath created to be received with thanksgiving of them which believe and know the truth."* (1 Timothy 4:1-3, KJV)

Seducing Spirit[1]

A seducing spirit refers to deceptive spiritual entities that lead people away from genuine Christian faith through misleading teachings, heresies, or false doctrines. These spirits are described as "seducing" because they wander, deceive, or entice believers into error, promoting ideas that contradict biblical truth.

The book of 1 Timothy is a pastoral epistle written by the Apostle Paul to his young protégé Timothy, who was overseeing the church in Ephesus. In this letter, Paul provides guidance on church organization, leadership, and doctrine. Chapter 4 shifts focus to warn against false teachings that would arise, emphasizing the importance of sound doctrine and godly living. This passage specifically addresses a prophecy about apostasy (departure from true faith) in the *"latter times."*

> *"Now the Spirit speaketh expressly, that in the latter times some shall depart from the faith, giving heed to **seducing spirits**, and doctrines of devils;"*

The first verse *"the Spirit speaketh expressly"*, indicating that Paul presents this as an explicit revelation from the Holy Spirit, underscoring its seriousness. In the latter days, individuals who once professed Christian faith abandon it. This applies to believers or professed believers who turn away, not outsiders initially. The cause of departure is following deceptive spiritual influences and their teachings. *"Seducing spirits"* are entities that entice through falsehoods, while *"doctrines of devils"* are demonic-originated ideas masquerading as truth.

---

1. Deceitful Spirits (NASB, ESV, CSB)
   Deceiving Spirit (NKJV, NIV)
   Deceptive Spirits (NLT)
   Seducing Spirit (KJV, YLT)

"Speaking lies in hypocrisy; having their conscience seared with a hot iron;"

In the second verse, the false teachers (implied as the mouthpieces of these spirits) promote falsehoods while pretending to be pious. Their hypocrisy involves insincere claims, often justified by a dulled moral sense. They have their *"conscience seared with a hot iron"* indicating a conscience burned and desensitized, making it insensitive to truth or guilt. Over time, repeated sin or deception hardens one's moral awareness, allowing unchecked promotion of error.

"Forbidding to marry, and commanding to abstain from meats, which God hath created to be received with thanksgiving of them which believe and know the truth."

In the third verse, Paul gives examples of demonic doctrines: prohibiting marriage or requiring abstinence from certain foods. Marriage is portrayed in Scripture as a divine institution from creation (Genesis 2:18-24), symbolizing Christ's relationship with the church (Ephesians 5:25-32). Forbidding it distorts God's design, turning a gift into a sin. *"Meats"* broadly means different types of foods, not just animal flesh. This echoes Old Testament dietary laws where certain foods were seen as defiling the spirit. Paul counters this in other letters, like Colossians 2:16-23, calling such rules *"self-imposed worship"* that lack value. True believers *"know the truth,"* which sanctifies creation's use. Thanksgiving and prayer consecrate these gifts.

Prayer for Those Who Have Drifted From Christianity

Heavenly Father,

I come before You lifting up ___________, who once walked in Your ways but has drifted away from the truth they professed. The Bible reveals that some who knew You turn aside, drawn by deceptive spiritual influences that contradict Your Word. Lord, I see how subtle lies and seemingly profound experiences can pull even the sincere away. Have mercy on ___________, and in Your compassion, expose the emptiness of these paths that lead them further from You.

I pray against the seducing spirits and demonic forces at work. Those evil influences that tempt through hypocritical voices and speak with charisma, promoting ideas that twist truth. Yet their own consciences have grown calloused, hiding personal failings behind moral posturing. Break through the deception surrounding ___________, reveal the hypocrisy that has dulled their discernment, and remind them of the genuine freedom and grace found only in following You.

Restore ___________'s heart to the solid foundation of biblical truth they once embraced. Awaken them from the gradual drift that made their departure feel natural and right. Guard them from further entanglement in these contradictory ideas. Draw them back with Your love, convicting them of sin and renewing their hunger for authentic relationship with Jesus. May Your Spirit work powerfully in their life so they may once again stand firm in Your unchanging truth.

In Jesus' name we pray,

Amen.

Prayer for Christians to Get Back to Church

Heavenly Father,

We come before You repenting for the complacency that has kept many believers at home instead of gathering in Your house, missing the vital fellowship, worship, and encouragement that comes from assembling with fellow believers. Stir within us a renewed conviction that church is not optional but essential for spiritual growth and unity in the body of Christ. Lord, break through the excuses that keep us isolated, and remind us that Your presence moves powerfully when Your people come together in one accord.

Gracious God, we pray that Your Spirit would convict hearts across our nation, transforming passive faith into active obedience. Let believers feel the gentle yet powerful prompting to step out of their homes and into houses of worship. Raise up a renewed passion for the body of Christ, where iron sharpens iron, burdens are shared, and Your love flows freely among us.

Lord, we cry out for this stirring to lead to a great revival of attendance and engagement, drawing wanderers back and strengthening the faithful to invite others. May Sundays become sacred times of encounter with You, not routines neglected, as Your Spirit moves mightily to unite and empower Your people for Your kingdom's work. Fill us with joy in obedience, and let our gatherings reflect the vibrant community You envision.

In Jesus' name we pray,

Amen.

Prayer Confronting Religions With Dietary Restrictions

Heavenly Father,

We come before You for those ensnared by religions that impose strict dietary restrictions, claiming such rules lead to holiness or favor with You. We recognize these commands as deceptive influences from seducing spirits that seek to bind people in legalism, turning them away from the freedom and grace found in the one true God. Lord, open eyes to see how these prohibitions twist Your generous provision of all foods for enjoyment and nourishment.

Gracious God, we pray that You would expose these false teachings across our nation, awakening consciences to the reality that any faith demanding abstinence from certain meats or foods does not reflect Your loving character. Help people discern the subtle seduction that promotes self-righteousness through rules, leading them to reject such doctrines and seek the liberty that comes from knowing You alone. Stir a hunger for authentic relationship with You, free from man-made burdens.

Lord, we cry out for a widespread turning, where those trapped in these restrictive religions find deliverance and embrace the one true God who created all things good. May Your Spirit convict and guide them to the joy of unrestricted fellowship with You, unhindered by deceptive commands that forbid what You have blessed.

In Jesus' name we pray,

Amen.

Rulers of the

Darkness of this

Age

OUTER DEMONIC INFLUENCES

*"We know that we are of God, and **the whole world lies under the sway of the wicked one**. And we know that the Son of God has come and has given us an understanding, that we may know Him who is true; and we are in Him who is true, in His Son Jesus Christ. This is the true God and eternal life. Little children, keep yourselves from idols."* (1 John 5:19-21)

Outer Demonic Influences

The Bible makes it clear that our struggle is not against flesh and blood, but against spiritual forces of evil (Ephesians 6:12). We all face powerful demonic influences that disrupts daily life. Influence often manifest from temptation, deception, oppression, and accusation.

Temptation exploits our natural desires, or *"works of the flesh"* such as *"adultery, fornication, uncleanness, lewdness, idolatry, sorcery, hatred, contentions, jealousies, outbursts of wrath, selfish ambitions, dissensions, heresies, envy, murders, drunkenness, revelries, and the like"* (Galatians 5:19-21). They operate through everyday circumstances that lead us to sin creating footholds that, if yielded to, erode our spiritual resolve and open doors to further oppression. Yet, as James 4:7 promises, submitting to God and resisting these temptations causes the devil to flee, empowering us through Christ's victory to choose righteousness over sin.

Demons are masters of lies, as Satan is called the *"father of lies"* (John 8:44). They excel as masters of deception by weaving falsehoods into the fabric of human thought and perception, often disguising their whispers as our own inner voice or rational justifications to lead us astray from God's truth. Through subtle manipulations, these spirits aim to erode faith, foster division, and blind people to spiritual realities, ultimately drawing them into bondage. Yet, the Bible equips believers to counter this with the belt of truth from the armor of God (Ephesians 6:14), discerning deception through prayer, the Word, and the Holy Spirit's guidance, ensuring that no lie can prevail against those anchored in Christ.

Demonic forces work through oppression and affliction by exerting external pressures that cause spiritual, emotional, mental, or physical distress, aiming to wear down individuals and hinder their faith without taking internal control. These spirits exploit vulnerabilities such as unrepented sin, bitterness, or generational patterns to amplify suffering and create strongholds of torment. Unforgiveness further invites these *"tormentors,"* as warned in the parable of the unforgiving servant (Matthew 18:34-35), manifesting as anxiety, relational strife, or unexplained ailments that erode joy and productivity. Yet, believers are empowered to overcome through submission to God, resistance in Jesus' name (James 4:7), and the assurance that no affliction can separate us from His love (Romans 8:38-39).

Accusation and division is the work of the devil, relentlessly exploiting human insecurities and relational fractures to sow discord, erode unity, and paralyze individuals with guilt. Satan is depicted as the *"accuser of the brethren"* who accuses believers day and night before God (Revelation 12:10). They amplify minor offenses into major rifts, stirring suspicion, gossip, or bitterness. This tactic not only weakens faith but also distracts from God's purposes. Nevertheless, be-lievers can counter this by embracing God's forgiveness, pursuing reconciliation (Matthew 5:23-24), and resisting the accuser through the blood of Christ, which silences every condemnation (Romans 8:1).

Demons pressure us into bad situations with the ultimate goal of possessing our bodies where their influence is much greater. Therefore when confronting Rulers of the Darkness of this Age, this prayer book is separated into evil spirits that war with us from the outside and evils spirits that torment us once they are on the inside. First, let's understand the spirits that grip our behaviors.

SPIRIT OF WEAKNESS

"To appoint to mourners in Zion, To give to them beauty instead of ashes, The oil of joy instead of mourning, A covering of praise for a **spirit of weakness**, *And He is calling to them, 'Trees of righteousness, The planting of Jehovah -- to be beautified.'"* (Isaiah 61:3, YLT)

Spirit of Weakness[1]

The spirit of weakness refers to a profound state of emotional, spiritual, and sometimes physical burden that afflicts individuals during times of mourning, grief, or oppression, often resulting from loss.

Being an Old Testament passage, this verse is a prophetic word about the coming of Jesus where God will comfort the Israelites. The Israelites experienced exile and destruction over the loss of their homeland and sacred sites when King Nebuchadnezzar conquered Judah. The exiles lived as captives in a foreign land feeling oppressed and were mourning their apparent abandonment by God due to curses of the law from their covenant unfaithfulness. Even when King Cyrus allowed some of them to return, the returnees encountered ruins, poverty, and opposition from neighbors. This ongoing hardship caused lingering sorrow as the rebuilt Jerusalem paled in comparison to its former splendor.

The prophecy conveys a divine exchange where God replaces symbols of grief and brokenness with ones of joy, honor, and strength. In their day, people would sprinkle ashes on their heads as a sign of deep mourning. But God promises to replace this with a *"crown of beauty"* (NIV). Anointing with *"oil"* was common for healing and here it counters the sorrow *"of mourning."* Mourners often wore sackcloth or torn garments to express grief. God exchanges these for a *"covering of praise"* that lifts their heavy spirits. The people, once broken, will become strong *"oaks of righteousness"* (NIV) rooted in strong standing with God to display His glory. The overall message is one of hope: God comforts the afflicted, turns tragedy into triumph, and rebuilds lives for His honor.

---

1. Disheartened Spirit (NASB)

   Faint Spirit (ESV)

   Spirit of Despair (NIV, NLT, CSB)

   Spirit of Heaviness (KJV, NKJV)

   Spirit of Weakness (YLT)

Comfort Me In My Grief

Heavenly Father,

You are the God of all comfort and I come to You right now with a heavy, aching heart. I am grieving ______________. The sorrow feels overwhelming, and I don't know how to carry it. My heart is broken and I feel so alone in this darkness.

Lord Jesus, You understand grief deeper than anyone. Draw near to me now as You promised. Wrap Your arms around me. Let me feel Your presence in a real, tangible way.

Holy Spirit, comfort me with Your peace. Guard my heart and mind. Quiet the racing thoughts. Give me strength for this moment, for today, and for the next. Help me breathe through the tears.

Replace my ashes with beauty, my mourning with the oil of joy, and my despair with a garment of praise. Even if I can't feel it yet, I ask You to plant seeds of hope in this sorrow. I know You are making all things new, that one day every tear will be wiped away.

Until then, hold me. Carry what I cannot carry. Whisper Your love when words fail. Surround me with Your people who can also provide comfort.

Thank You that You never leave me or forsake me. Thank You that this grief cannot separate me from Your love in Christ Jesus.

I trust You with my broken heart. Fill me with Your comfort so that one day I can comfort others with the comfort You've given me.

In Jesus' name,

Amen.

I Feel so Much Sadness

Heavenly Father,

Right now my heart feels so sad. I don't even know how to explain it all, but You see every part of it. You know the ache I'm carrying.

I'm coming to You because I have nowhere else to go. Please come close. Sit with me in this sadness. Let me feel that You're really here, even if it's just a quiet sense that I'm not completely alone.

Jesus, You cried real tears. You felt deep sorrow. You understand this better than anyone. Wrap Your arms around me. Comfort me the way only You can; softly, gently, without rushing me to "get over it."

Holy Spirit, breathe peace into this hurt. Calm the storm inside me, even if the sadness doesn't leave right away. Give me strength to make it through the next hour, the next day. Help me breathe when it feels hard to breathe.

Remind me that this sadness isn't forever. You see the end of the story. You promise joy in the morning, beauty for ashes, and that one day every tear will be wiped away. Help me hold onto that hope, even when it feels small.

Thank You that You never leave me, even when I feel abandoned. Thank You that You love me on my worst, saddest days. Thank You that You're already working in this pain, even when I can't see it.

Please stay near. Carry me when I can't walk. Whisper Your love when everything else is quiet.

In Jesus' name,

Amen.

Hopelessness Surrounds Me

Heavenly Father,

I feel completely hopeless right now. Everything looks dark and impossible. My heart is heavy, my thoughts are stuck in despair, and I can't see any way forward. It feels like nothing will ever get better, like I'm forgotten or too broken to fix.

But You see me in this place. You know every tear, every sigh, every "why" in my mind. You are the God who never leaves, the One who is close to the broken-hearted and saves those crushed in spirit. Come near to me now, let me sense Your presence, even faintly.

Lord Jesus, You felt the weight of despair in the garden. You understand this darkness better than anyone. Hold me when I can't hold on. Be my hope when I have none left. Renew my mind with Your truth.

Holy Spirit, breathe fresh hope into my soul. Stir faith where it's died. Help me trust You one breath at a time. Give me strength for today; grace to get up, to eat, to reach out, to keep going. Anchor me in You, the sure and steadfast hope.

I confess this hopelessness feels bigger than You right now. Forgive my unbelief and help my unbelief. Lift my eyes to You, the God of all comfort. Restore joy where it's been stolen. Remind me that my story isn't finished, that morning comes after the night.

Thank You that nothing, not this despair, not my feelings, can separate me from Your love in Christ Jesus. Thank You that You are faithful even when I feel faithless. Thank You for holding me when I can't hold on.

In Jesus' name,

Amen.

Release Me From Depression

Heavenly Father,

I come to You feeling heavy, dark, and overwhelmed. Depression has settled over me like a thick fog. I feel numb, hopeless, tired, worthless, and alone. My thoughts are racing or stuck in despair, and I don't know how to climb out. But I know You see me. You are the God who is near to the brokenhearted and saves those who are crushed in spirit. You have not abandoned me.

Lord Jesus, You wept in sorrow and felt the weight of anguish in the garden. You understand this pain better than anyone. Draw close to me right now. Let me sense Your presence even when I feel nothing.

Holy Spirit, fill me with Your peace that surpasses understanding. Guard my heart and mind. Renew my thoughts, replace lies with Your truth. Help me take every dark thought captive. Give me strength for this moment and hope for tomorrow.

Lift this heaviness, Lord. Restore to me the joy of Your salvation. Even if joy feels far away, plant seeds of it in my heart. Remind me that You are my light in this darkness, my rock when everything shakes.

I confess any sin, unbelief, or bitterness that's feeding this, forgive me and cleanse me. Help me trust You one breath at a time. Surround me with Your people who can encourage, pray, and walk with me.

Thank You that nothing can separate me from Your love in Christ Jesus. Thank You that You are making all things new, and one day every tear will be wiped away. Until then, hold me, carry what I cannot. Whisper Your love when I'm in need.

In Jesus' name,

Amen.

In This Moment I Am Overwhelmed

Heavenly Father,

I feel so overwhelmed right now. Everything is piling up too high, too fast, and I can't catch my breath. The weight of ____________ is crushing me. My mind is spinning, my heart is racing, and I don't know where to start or how to keep going.

But You see it all. You know every detail of this chaos. You are my refuge and strength, an ever-present help in trouble. I run to You now, hide me under Your wings. Help me feel Your steady hand in this storm.

Lord Jesus, You calmed the raging sea with a word. Speak peace over my overwhelmed soul. Take this burden from my shoulders, it's too heavy for me to carry alone. Teach me to cast all my cares on You because You care for me. Order my steps when I can't see the path. Give me wisdom for the next right thing, strength for the next hour, and grace just for today.

Holy Spirit, breathe calm into my chaos. Quiet the noise in my head. Fill me with Your peace that surpasses understanding. Guard my heart and mind in Christ Jesus. Help me release what I can't control and trust You with what I can.

Thank You that You're not overwhelmed by my overwhelm. Thank You that Your yoke is easy and Your burden is light. Thank You that in You, I can do all things through Christ who strengthens me.

Hold me close until the waves settle. Be my anchor today.

In Jesus' name,

Amen.

Heal My Aching Heart

Heavenly Father,

My heart is aching so deeply right now, it feels shattered, heavy, and hard to breathe through. The pain of ___________ is overwhelming, and I don't know how to carry it alone.

But You see every tear, You collect them in Your bottle, and You are near to the brokenhearted. You save those whose spirits are crushed. Draw close to me now, let me feel Your presence wrapping around me like a shield.

Lord Jesus, You know heartache. You wept, You felt betrayal, You carried the weight of the world's sorrow on the cross. Walk with me in this valley. Hold my broken heart in Your hands. Heal the wounds that feel too deep to mend. Bind them up as You promised, and slowly replace this grief with Your peace.

Holy Spirit, come and fill the empty spaces. Soothe the raw places. Quiet the racing thoughts and the "what ifs." Give me strength for today, one breath, one step at a time. Help me trust that You are working even in this pain, weaving something good, and that joy can return in the morning.

Help me release what I need to let go of. Teach me to forgive as You forgave, and to rest in Your love that never fails. Surround me with Your people who can weep with me and remind me of truth.

Thank You that nothing can separate me from Your love. Thank You that You are making all things new, and one day every tear will be wiped away. Until then, carry me. Renew my hope. Restore my soul.

In Jesus' name,

Amen.

Haughty Spirit

*"Pride goes before destruction, And a **haughty spirit** before a fall. Better to be of a humble spirit with the lowly, Than to divide the spoil with the proud."* (Proverbs 16:18-19)

Haughty Spirit[1]

A haughty or arrogant spirit refers to an attitude of excessive self-importance, superiority, and disdain for others, often rooted in self-deception and independence from God. This mindset initially fosters certain empowering but misguided feelings, but it inevitably leads to downfall, triggering a range of negative emotional experiences as a consequence.

"Pride goes before destruction, And a haughty spirit before a fall."

Solomon was renowned for his God-given wisdom. His Proverbs are a compilation of sayings as instructional wisdom to guide moral living and do not reference a particular story in the Bible. The core of this message is excessive pride inevitably leads to downfall, humiliation, or ruin, while humility offers protection and honor. This verse is part of a larger contrast in Proverbs between the wise (humble) and foolish (proud) with the next verse stating,

"Better to be of humble spirit with the lowly, than to divide the spoil with the proud."

This verse reinforces that humility brings wisdom, honor, and life, whereas pride invites disgrace and discipline. Pride represents independence from God, contrasting with *"the fear of the Lord"* (read my book *The Secret of the Lord* to learn more) which is the beginning of wisdom (Proverbs 9:10). Similar themes appear elsewhere in Proverbs:

---

1. Arrogant Spirit (CSB)
   Haughty Spirit (KJV, YLT, NASB, NIV, NKJV, ESV)
   Haughtiness (NLT)

"When pride comes, then comes shame; But with the humble is wisdom." (Proverbs 11:2)

"Before destruction the heart of a man is haughty, And before honor is humility." (Proverbs 18:12)

"A man's pride will bring him low, But the humble in spirit will retain honor." (Proverbs 29:23)

In prayer, we may seek God's help to cultivate a lowly spirit, guarding against the pitfalls of arrogance to walk in His favor.

Release Me From My Prideful Ways

Heavenly Father,

I come to You right now aware that pride has taken root in my heart, and I need Your help to be free. I've relied on myself instead of You. I confess that pride has blinded me and kept me from fully depending on You.

Lord, search my heart. Expose every trace of pride, every hidden attitude, every moment I've exalted myself, every refusal to bow. Bring it into the light so I can see it clearly and turn from it.

I repent of my prideful ways. Forgive me for every time I've acted as if I didn't need You or as if my way was best. I turn from self-exaltation and ask You to break its power over me. Crush my pride Lord, so that I can walk in true humility.

Holy Spirit, fill me with a humble heart like Christ's, who humbled Himself to the point of death on a cross. Teach me to esteem others better than myself. Give me eyes to see my own smallness before Your greatness and to rejoice in serving rather than being served. Replace pride with gratitude, entitlement with thankfulness, comparison with contentment.

Thank You that You resist the proud but give grace to the humble. Thank You that You are patient with me and faithful to complete the good work You've begun. Thank You that in Christ I am already accepted, not because I'm humble enough, but because He was humble enough for me.

Keep humbling me, Lord. Don't let me stay comfortable in pride. Lead me lower so I can be lifted up by Your hand. Make me more like Jesus every day.

In Jesus' name,

Amen.

My Vanity Made Me Drift Far From You

Heavenly Father,

I come to You convicted of my vain ways. I confess I've been too focused on my appearance, status, achievements, and what others think of me. I've focused on things that feed my pride, seeking to impress people rather than honor You.

Lord, this vanity is sin in Your sight. It has stolen glory that belongs only to You, distracted me from true worship, and hindered selfless love for others. I am truly sorry. I repent of every vain thought, every moment I exalted my image over Your name, and every time I sought human praise instead of pleasing You.

Forgive me, God. Wash me clean through the blood of Jesus Christ, who humbled Himself so I could be forgiven. I claim Your promise: if I confess my sins, You are faithful and just to forgive me and cleanse me from all unrighteousness. I receive that full forgiveness now, not because I deserve it, but because Jesus paid the price.

Holy Spirit, come and do a deep work in my heart. Root out vanity wherever it hides. Replace my craving for human approval with a deeper hunger for Yours. Teach me to see myself as You see me.

Help me walk in freedom from vanity today. When old patterns return, quickly convict me so I can confess and turn back to You. Let my life reflect a heart fixed on You, not on self.

Thank You for Your mercy that covers even this sin, for loving me when I was vain, and for the cross where my pride was crucified with Christ. Thank You for making me new and more like Jesus every day.

In Jesus' name,

Amen.

I Need to Be More Empathetic

Heavenly Father,

I come to You in the name of Jesus, grateful for Your compassion toward me, even when I was far from You. You see my heart fully, and I confess that I have often lacked empathy for others. I've been indifferent to their pain, quick to judge instead of understand, cold when people needed warmth, or too focused on myself to truly care about what others are going through.

Forgive me, Lord, for every time I've failed to reflect Your tender heart. Forgive me for the ways this has hurt people around me and grieved Your Spirit. I repent of this hardness. I don't want to live with a calloused or numb heart anymore.

Soften my heart, Father. Break through any walls I've built from past hurts from pride, fear, or selfishness. Remove numbness and replace it with tenderness and genuine feeling. Give me eyes to see people as You see them and move me with real compassion like Jesus did.

Fill me with Your Holy Spirit so that empathy and love become natural in me. Help me listen without interrupting, feel without being overwhelmed, and respond with kindness and patience. Teach me to bear others' burdens, weep with those who weep, and show mercy as freely as You've shown it to me.

Thank You that You are faithful to forgive and transform me into the image of Your Son. I receive Your forgiveness right now and trust You to do this deep heart work over time. Give me opportunities today to practice empathy, even in small ways, and grace when I stumble.

In Jesus' name,

Amen.

I Don't Want to Live Independently From You Anymore

Heavenly Father,

I come to You with a weary heart. For too long I have lived independently of You, making decisions on my own, relying on my own strength, chasing my own plans, leaning on my own understanding, and treating You as an optional part of my life. I have pushed You to the side and trusted myself more than You.

Lord, I am tired of that way of living. It has left me disconnected from the peace and purpose You give. I don't want to live like that anymore. I don't want to keep walking alone, carrying burdens You never asked me to carry, or making choices without Your wisdom.

Right now, I choose to stop living independently of You. I repent of every time I have relied on myself instead of on You. Forgive me for my pride, my self-sufficiency, and my rebellion. Wash me clean by the blood of Jesus.

Fill me with Your Holy Spirit so I never drift back into independence from You. Help me to depend on You completely. Let my life be marked by constant communion with You, not occasional check-ins.

Thank You for Your patience with me. Thank You that You never gave up on me. Thank You for welcoming me back with open arms. Thank you for the promise that if I draw near to You, You will draw near to me.

From this day forward, I choose dependence on You. I want nothing more than to walk closely with You every single day. I receive Your nearness right now.

In Jesus' name,

Amen.

Spirit of Bondage

*"For you did not receive the **spirit of bondage** again to fear, but you received the Spirit of adoption by whom we cry out, 'Abba, Father.'"*
(Romans 8:15)

Spirit of Bondage[1]

In this verse, the Bible contrasts the spirit of bondage with the Spirit of adoption received by believers as God's children. This refers to a spiritual condition of fear and enslavement, often tied to living under the weight of sin where we feel distant from God.

When we sin, shame often overwhelms us, and Satan exploits this vulnerability to create a sense of distance from God, effectively enslaving us to our wrongdoing. This spirit hinders us from approaching Him as a loving Father, instead portraying Him as a remote and severe judge. We might feel compelled to earn back His favor through our own efforts, much like mending broken human relationships. But God operates differently, extending grace beyond our striving.

Sin stirs up deep guilt and hopelessness, and under this spirit of bondage, we may encounter timidity in prayer, a wavering sense of assurance, or a burdensome duty to obey driven by fear rather than love. Such emotions foster spiritual unrest and a barrier to intimate fellowship with God. Yet, for believers, this bondage is not an endpoint; it acts as a necessary prelude, contrasting sharply with the freeing Spirit of adoption. Here, fear dissolves into the heartfelt cry of *"Abba, Father!"* In prayer, by acknowledging and renouncing this spirit through repentance, we unlock true freedom and rediscover joy in God's abiding presence.

---

1. Spirit of Bondage (KJV, YLT, NKJV)
    Spirit of Slavery (NASB, ESV, CSB)
    Spirit that makes you fearful (NLT)
    Spirit you received (NIV)

I Feel Unworthy of Your Love

Heavenly Father,

I come to You right now feeling so unworthy of Your love. My heart tells me I'm not enough. These thoughts make me want to hide from You instead of running to You. But I know that's not what You want.

Lord, forgive me for believing lies about Your love instead of trusting what Your Word says. Forgive me for measuring Your affection by my performance or how I feel about myself. I repent of letting shame or self-rejection push me away from the arms You've opened wide.

Thank You that Your love isn't based on my worthiness, it's based on Your unchanging character and the finished work of Jesus on the cross. Thank You that while I was still a sinner, Christ died for me. Thank You that You lavished Your love on me and call me Your child. Thank You that nothing can separate me from Your love.

Help me believe this deep in my soul, Father. When I feel inadequate, flood my heart with the reality of how wide and long and high and deep Your love for me is. Quiet the accusing voices and let me hear You rejoicing over me with singing. Help me receive Your love, not as something I have to deserve, but as a gift You've already given.

Draw me close. Let me rest in Your delight over me, even when I don't like myself. Teach me to abide in Your love daily, to let it heal these feelings of unworthiness over time. Give me grace to come to You boldly, just as I am, knowing You welcome me.

In Jesus' name,

Amen.

My Guilt Makes Me Want to Hide

Heavenly Father,

I come to You right now, even though guilt is screaming that I'm not welcome, that I'm too far gone, that I should stay away. This weight keeps me from praying, from reading Your Word, from believing You still want me close. I confess that I've let this guilt define me more than Your grace.

Lord Jesus, You know every sin, every failure, every moment I've fallen short, and You still died for me. I believe You took all my guilt on the cross, and when You said *"It is finished,"* You meant it. Yet my heart hasn't fully believed or received that freedom. Forgive me for doubting Your full forgiveness and for letting shame win instead of Your truth.

Break this cycle, God. Silence the accusing voices that say I'm too far gone or that I have to earn my way back. Remind me that there is no condemnation for those in Christ Jesus. Help me trust that You are faithful and just to forgive my sins and cleanse me from all unrighteousness when I confess.

Lift this burden off me. Replace the guilt with the peace that comes from knowing I'm fully accepted in You. Give me courage to approach You daily, even when I feel down, because that's when I need You most. Draw me close anyway.

Holy Spirit, convict me where I still need to repent, but comfort me with the assurance of forgiveness. Help me walk in the reality that my sins are remembered no more. I receive Your mercy right now.

In Jesus' name,

Amen.

My Past Keeps Me Away From You

Heavenly Father,

Right now I feel so condemned by my past. Memories of what I did, what I said, how I failed, keep rising up and accusing me. I feel unworthy, like I'll never be free of this weight. The shame is loud, and it's hard to believe I'm really forgiven.

But Your Word says something different. It says there is no condemnation for those who are in Christ Jesus. It says if I confess my sins, You are faithful and just to forgive me and cleanse me. It says You have removed my transgressions. It says Jesus became sin for me so that I might become the righteousness of God in Him.

Lord Jesus, I bring every accusing memory, every regret, every moment I'm ashamed of, and I lay them at Your cross. I believe You paid for them fully: past, present, and future. I receive Your forgiveness right now, not because I feel it, but because You promised it. Wash me clean with Your blood. Silence the accuser.

Holy Spirit, come and testify to me that I am a child of God. Replace the voice of condemnation with Your voice of love and acceptance. Help me believe I am forgiven, accepted, and delighted in. Lift this heavy shame off my shoulders. Give me the peace of knowing I'm no longer under judgment.

Thank You, Father, that You don't keep a record of my wrongdoings. Thank You that when You look at me, You see Jesus' righteousness. Thank You that my past doesn't define me, You do.

Help me walk today in the freedom You've already given. When old accusations rise, remind me to run back to this truth.

In Jesus' name,

Amen.

Remove the Shame That I Feel

Heavenly Father,

I come before You weighed down with heavy shame. It makes me afraid to approach You. It whispers that I'm too far gone, that I've disqualified myself from Your presence. It keeps me hiding instead of running into Your arms.

Lord, I confess whatever is fueling this shame, that these were wrong, and I repent. But I also confess that I've let shame define me more than Your forgiveness does. Forgive me for doubting Your mercy and for staying away when You've invited me near.

Thank You, Jesus, that You took my shame on the cross. That You were despised and rejected so I could be accepted. Thank You that You blot out my transgressions and remember my sins no more. Thank You that You promise to remove shame and replace it with praise and honor.

Right now, I ask You to take this shame away. Lift it off me like a heavy garment. Strip away every robe of reproach and clothe me instead with garments of salvation. Roll away this stone that's blocking my path to You. Heal the wounds that feed it. Silence the accusing voices and let me hear Your delight over me.

Draw me closer, Father. Give me boldness to seek You without hesitation, even when old feelings try to pull me back. Replace shame with the joy of knowing I'm fully loved and fully forgiven. Help me walk in freedom today.

Thank You for hearing this prayer and for already beginning to lift this burden. I receive Your cleansing and Your nearness right now.

In Jesus' name,

Amen.

SPIRIT OF JEALOUSY

*"'If any man's wife goes astray and behaves unfaithfully toward him...and it is hidden from the eyes of her husband...if the **spirit of jealousy** comes upon him and he becomes jealous of his wife, who has defiled herself; or she has not defiled herself—then the man shall bring his wife to the priest.' The priest shall take holy water in an earthen vessel, and take some of the dust that is on the floor of the tabernacle and put it into the water. And the priest shall put her under oath, and say to the woman, 'If no man has lain with you...be free from this bitter water that brings a curse. But if you have gone astray...the Lord make you a curse and an oath among your people...may this water that causes the curse go into your stomach, and make your belly swell and your thigh rot.' But if the woman has not defiled herself, and is clean, then she shall be free and may conceive children."* (Numbers 5:12-28)

Spirit of Jealousy[1]

The spirit of jealousy appears exclusively in the Old Testament within the context of a ritual law concerning suspected marital infidelity. Numbers 5 outlines a divine ordeal to address a husband's suspicion of his wife's infidelity when no witnesses or direct evidence exist. This law is presented as part of God's instructions to Moses for maintaining ritual purity and holiness within the Israelite camp after their exodus from Egypt. As the Israelites camped at Mount Sinai, they received laws to structure their society as a covenant people under God.

In ancient Israelite culture, adultery was viewed as a grave offense often equated with spiritual unfaithfulness to God. Without this ritual, a jealous husband might resort to violence, arbitrary divorce, or social ostracism. The spirit of jealousy is portrayed as an intense emotional state that overwhelms the husband, prompting the need for resolution to prevent ongoing strife.

The ritual's purpose shifted judgment from human hands to divine intervention, protecting potentially innocent women from false accusations in a time when they had limited legal recourse. It allowed for marital reconciliation by "clearing" the wife if innocent or punishing her if found guilty, and it absolved the husband of guilt for baseless suspicion, enabling him to remain with his wife.

The woman had to drink *"bitter water"* (holy water mixed with tabernacle dust) in a temple setting which relied on divine intervention to reveal guilt or innocence. This parallels the golden calf incident in Exodus 32 where the idolaters drank water with ground idol dust symbolizing judgment of spiritual idolatry against God who was a jealous husband when the Israelites were unfaithful to Him.

---

1. Attitude of Jealousy (NASB)

   Feelings of Jealousy (NIV, NLT - becomes jealous, CSB)

   Spirit of Jealousy (KJV, YLT, NKJV, ESV)

I Confess My Jealousy of Others

Heavenly Father,

I come to You confessing my jealousy and envy. It rises up when I see others succeeding, being blessed, or having what I long for. It makes me bitter, discontent, and focused on lack instead of Your goodness. I've compared myself, coveted what isn't mine, and let these feelings poison my heart and steal my joy.

Lord, forgive me. I repent of harboring envy and letting it grow into resentment or strife. I know it's not from You, it's a work of the flesh that grieves Your Spirit. Forgive me for doubting Your perfect plan for my life and for not trusting that You are good and generous toward me.

Thank You that love does not envy, and that You are growing that love in me. Thank You that You provide a way out of temptation. Thank You for the unique path You've designed for me. Help me stop looking sideways and start looking to You.

Holy Spirit, convict me quickly when jealousy stirs and help me turn it into prayer. Replace envy with gratitude. Open my eyes to the blessings You've already poured out on me. Guard my heart from comparison. Give me a heart that celebrates others without feeling diminished. Teach me to be content in every circumstance, trusting Your timing and provision.

Thank You for hearing me, for forgiving me completely, and for working in me to produce the fruit of the Spirit. I receive Your help right now to walk free from jealousy.

In Jesus' name,

Amen.

I Have Been Falsely Accused

Heavenly Father,

I come to You right now, deeply hurt and burdened by false accusations. People are saying things about me that aren't true. It feels unfair, unjust, and overwhelming. The pain of being misunderstood and wrongly judged is heavy, and part of me wants to defend myself fiercely or lash out.

Lord, You see everything clearly. You know my heart, my actions, and every detail they don't. You are the God of truth who cannot lie and who hates false witness. I bring this whole situation to You and lay it at Your feet. Expose the lies and bring the truth to light in Your perfect way and time. Let no weapon formed against me prosper, and silence every accusing tongue.

Help me not to repay evil for evil or take matters into my own hands. Give me grace to entrust justice to You. Guard my heart from bitterness, resentment, and despair. If there's any area where I've fallen short or need to repent, show me and help me make it right.

Strengthen me to respond like Jesus. When He was reviled, He didn't revile in return. When falsely accused, He entrusted Himself to You. Give me wisdom in what to say or not say, courage to stand in truth without defensiveness, and peace that surpasses understanding as I wait on You.

Thank You that You are my refuge and strength, a very present help in trouble. Thank You that the truth will prevail because You are the Judge who never errs. I trust You to work this for good, even when I can't see how.

In Jesus' name,

Amen.

Paranoia Has Damaged My Relationships

Heavenly Father,

I come to You with feelings of suspicion and paranoia. My mind races with doubts about people's intentions, hidden motives, or threats that may not even be real. It makes me guarded, isolated, quick to assume the worst, and it steals my peace. These thoughts exhaust me and pull me away from trusting You and others as I should.

Lord, forgive me for letting fear and suspicion rule my thoughts instead of Your truth. Forgive me for not casting my cares on You sooner and for assuming the worst rather than believing the best. I repent of any distrust that dishonors You or hurts to relationships You've placed in my life.

Help me right now, God. Take these paranoid thoughts captive and make them obedient to Christ. Renew my mind with Your truth. Help me discern real concerns from unfounded fears. Give me wisdom to know when caution is healthy and when suspicion is harmful. You are in control, nothing catches You by surprise, and You work all things for good.

Teach me to pray instead of worry. To bring every anxious thought to You immediately. Give me boldness like a lion, not fleeing from shadows. Guard my heart from bitterness or isolation; help me build healthy, trusting relationships grounded in You.

Thank You for hearing me, for forgiving me, and for already working to set my mind free. I receive Your peace and sound mind today. Keep pulling me back to You when suspicion rises.

In Jesus' name,

Amen.

I Can't Face This Exclusion Anymore

Heavenly Father,

I feel so ostracized right now, left out, excluded, overlooked, and rejected by people whose acceptance I longed for. It hurts deeply; it makes me question my worth and want to pull away from everyone. The loneliness is heavy, and part of me wonders if something's wrong with me or if I'll always be on the outside.

Lord, thank You that You see me when no one else does. You know every detail of this pain, and You never reject or abandon Your children. Thank You that I'm never truly alone because You are with me wherever I go.

Forgive me for any ways I've let this rejection define me more than Your love does. Forgive the bitterness that's crept in toward those who have excluded me. Heal the wounds this has caused in my heart.

Comfort me, God. Draw near to my broken heart. Replace the sting of rejection with the security of Your unchanging acceptance. Give me courage to keep loving others even when it's not returned, and grace to forgive those who've hurt me. Open doors to genuine, godly connections where I can belong and be valued.

Help me shine Your light even in this loneliness. Use it to make me more compassionate toward others who feel left out. Remind me daily that my ultimate belonging is in You, and that no exclusion on earth can change how precious I am to You.

Thank You for being my refuge and the One who turns mourning into joy. I trust You to carry me through this and bring good from it.

In Jesus' name,

Amen.

SPIRIT OF FEAR

*"Therefore I remind you to stir up the gift of God which is in you through the laying on of my hands. For God has not given us a **spirit of fear**, but of power and of love and of a sound mind."* (2 Timothy 1:6-7)

Spirit of Fear[1]

The spirit of fear refers to a disposition or influence not given by God, contrasting with the spirit of power, love, and sound mind that He provides. It's not just a fleeting emotion but a controlling force that can dominate thoughts, actions, and relationships, leading individuals away from God's purpose and into a state of spiritual paralysis.

The spirit of fear manifests in multifaceted ways, impacting our emotional, mental, spiritual, and even physical well-being. It operates subtly at first, often masquerading as caution or realism, but escalates to create cycles of negativity and limitation. In essence, the spirit of fear acts as a thief, robbing us of the abundant life promised in Scripture by replacing God's empowerment with chains of intimidation.

The 2 Timothy 1:6-7 verse is part of a letter from the Apostle Paul to his young disciple Timothy. Paul was imprisoned in Rome awaiting execution and he wrote to Timothy, who was pastoring the church in Ephesus. At the time there was intense Roman persecution of Christians under Emperor Nero. Nero targeted Christians, leading to widespread arrests, torture, and executions. Believers faced public spectacles of cruelty, such as being burned alive or thrown to wild animals. This created an atmosphere of terror, making public faith declarations risky and fostering fear among early Christians.

Timothy, described as young and possibly naturally timid (inferred from Paul's earlier encouragements in 1 Timothy 4:12), was dealing with internal church issues like false teachers spreading heresy and causing division. Additionally, associating with Paul, a known prisoner, could invite shame or danger. Paul notes

---

1. Spirit of Fear (KJV, YLT, NKJV, ESV, CSB)
   Spirit of Fear and Timidity (NLT)
   Spirit of Timidity (NASB)
   Timid (NIV)

in the chapter that some had abandoned him out of fear (2 Timothy 1:15), and he urges Timothy not to be ashamed of the gospel or of Paul himself.

From his dungeon, Paul reminds Timothy to *"stir up"* the spiritual gift received through the laying on of hands, implying that fear was quenching Timothy's zeal. The spirit of fear likely stemmed from these combined pressures: external threats of persecution, internal doubts, and the human tendency toward self-preservation. Paul counters this by pointing to God's provision, encouraging Timothy (and by extension, all believers) to rely on divine strength for bold ministry amid adversity.

Anxiety is Crushing Me

Heavenly Father,

I come to You right now with this heavy, racing anxiety pressing on my chest. My mind won't stop spinning, fears of what might happen, what-ifs that keep replaying, physical tension, restlessness, dread that steals my peace and joy. It feels like a storm inside me, and I can't quiet it on my own.

Lord, I've let these anxious thoughts grow bigger than Your promises. I've tried to control things I can't control and it's only made the storm louder. Forgive me for every time I've leaned on my own understanding instead of trusting You.

Thank You that You are the God of peace. Thank You that I do not have to be anxious about anything, but can bring every concern to You in prayer, and Your peace will guard my heart and my mind. Thank You that You have not given me a spirit of fear, but of power, love, and a sound mind.

Right now, I cast every anxious thought, every fear, every worry at Your feet. Take them, Lord, I can't carry them anymore. Replace this churning anxiety with Your perfect peace. Quiet my racing mind. Steady my breathing. Calm my body. Let Your presence wrap around me like a shield.

Help me fix my thoughts. Teach me to breathe in Your truth and breathe out the fear. Strengthen me when I feel weak. Fill me with Your Holy Spirit so I walk in power instead of panic.

Thank You for being near me in this storm. Thank You for hearing every worried thought I haven't even put into words. Thank You that You are already working, even when I can't see it yet. I receive Your peace right now.

In Jesus' name,

Amen.

I Feel Intimidated

Heavenly Father,

I come to You right now feeling intimidated. It makes my heart race, my confidence shrink, and my voice feel weak. I feel inadequate, afraid of failing, of being judged, of not measuring up. I want to hide or run, but I know You have not called me to fear.

Lord, forgive me for the times I've looked at the size of the problem instead of the size of my God. Forgive me for letting intimidation steal my courage and keep me from stepping forward in faith. I repent of trusting my feelings more than Your promises.

Thank You that You are with me. Thank You that You have not given me a spirit of fear, but of power, love, and a sound mind. Thank You that You are my refuge and strength, a very present help in trouble.

Right now, I ask You to lift this intimidation off me. Replace it with Your courage. Fill me with the boldness that comes from knowing You are greater than anything that intimidates me.

Help me see every intimidating situation through Your eyes, not as giants, but as opportunities to trust You more. Strengthen me in this moment. Give me the grace to take the next step, to say the next word, to face what feels too big. Remind me that You are my defender, my shield, my strength, and my victory.

Thank You for never leaving me to face anything alone. Thank You that in You I am more than a conqueror. I receive Your courage, Your peace, and Your strength right now.

In Jesus' name,

Amen.

Help Me With My Doubt and Unbelief

Heavenly Father,

I come to You weary from these negative thoughts and waves of doubt and unbelief that flood my mind. They tell me lies. They exhaust me, steal my joy, and make it hard to believe Your promises. I don't want these thoughts to control me anymore.

Lord, forgive me for entertaining doubts or believing lies instead of Your truth. Search my heart right now, reveal any roots of unbelief, fear, bitterness, or old wounds feeding these thoughts. I repent and ask You to cleanse me.

Thank You that You are greater than any thought or doubt. Thank You for the mind of Christ and for not giving me a spirit of fear but of power, love, and a sound mind. Thank You that I can take every thought captive to obey Christ and be transformed by renewing my mind in Your Word.

Help me now, God. Silence the negative voices and replace them with Your truth. When doubt whispers, remind me of Your faithfulness. Fill my mind with what is true and right. Give me perfect peace as I fix my thoughts on You.

Holy Spirit, guard my mind today. Help me recognize lies quickly and counter them with Scripture. Draw me deeper into Your Word so truth crowds out negativity. Strengthen me to choose gratitude and trust even when feelings lag behind.

Thank You for fighting for my mind and for the victory already won in Jesus. I receive Your peace, clarity, and renewed thinking right now. Keep renewing me day by day.

In Jesus' name,

Amen.

I Want to Surrender to Your Will

Heavenly Father,

I come before You today wanting to surrender fully to Your will, but I confess it's hard. Parts of me still want my way, my plans, my timing, my comfort, my understanding. I hold onto control because I'm afraid of what letting go might mean. Forgive me for resisting You and for leaning on my own understanding instead of trusting Yours.

Lord Jesus, thank You for modeling perfect surrender in the Garden. When facing the cross, You prayed, *"Not my will, but Yours be done."* Thank You that Your will is always good, pleasing, and perfect. Thank You that You are trustworthy and loving. You work all things for good for those who love You.

Help me surrender right now. I lay down my desires, my fears, and my need to know the "why" or "how." Take my past regrets, present struggles, and future unknowns, and align it with Your perfect plan. Soften my heart where it's stubborn; break any idols of control, comfort, or self-reliance. Renew my mind so I can discern and delight in Your will.

Give me grace to say "yes" to You daily. When resistance rises, remind me of Your faithfulness and draw me back to trust. Fill me with Your peace that surpasses understanding as I release what I can't carry. Help me live as a living sacrifice, holy and pleasing to You.

Thank You for inviting me into this surrender, not as a burden, but as freedom and intimacy with You. I receive Your strength to let go and follow wherever You lead.

In Jesus' name,

Amen.

Rulers of the Darkness of This Age

Demonic Spirits that Possess Us

*"And Jesus went about all Galilee, teaching in their synagogues, preaching the gospel of the kingdom, and healing all kinds of sickness and all kinds of disease among the people. Then His fame went throughout all Syria; and they brought to Him all sick people who were afflicted with various diseases and torments, and those who were **demon-possessed**, epileptics, and paralytics; and He healed them.'"* (Mark 4:23-24)

Demonic Spirits that Possess Us

In the Old Testament, there are no accounts of demons or evil spirits being cast out from people in the manner of exorcisms such as those performed by Jesus and His disciples in the New Testament. The reason for this is man lost authority of the earth given to him in Genesis when Adam ate the fruit from the Tree of Knowledge of Good and Evil. When Adam sinned, Satan stole authority of the world from man. However, early on in Jesus' earthly ministry, He gave authority back to the disciples,

"And when He had called His twelve disciples to Him, He gave them power over unclean spirits, to cast them out, and to heal all kinds of sickness and all kinds of disease." (Matthew 10:1)

Jesus, as the second member of the Holy Trinity, had authority over demons because He was God in the flesh walking on the earth. He was able to grant these powers to the disciples. Interestingly, when Jesus was being tempted by Satan for 40 days, if Jesus would have bowed His knee to Satan, Satan would have taken power and authority over God which was always his end goal, to be higher than God. This is why angels were constantly ministering to Jesus during His time of weakness, there was a lot at stake!

The Bible describes humans as consisting of spirit, soul, and body,

"Now may the God of peace Himself sanctify you completely; and may your whole spirit, soul, and body be preserved blameless at the coming of our Lord Jesus Christ." (1 Thessalonians 5:23)

The Holy Spirit is inside every single person but He does not get awakened until a person becomes born again. So the question is, if Christians are filled with the Holy Spirit, can they still inhabit demonic spirits? If it were impossible for a believer to be filled with the Holy Spirit while still having demonic spirits present, then those demons would automatically be forced to leave the moment of salvation. However, that doesn't typically occur, demonic influences often remain.

The Holy Spirit is God inside of us and is what leads and guides us through the challenges of life. Our soul is what goes to heaven or hell. Demons are restricted to operating in the soul and body of a Christian, but not in the regenerated spirit, where the Holy Spirit resides. Demons target and afflict the soul's areas like emotions, thoughts, and decisions, as well as the physical body, but they cannot inhabit or control the spirit of a true believer.

As Christians mature and draw closer to Jesus, there's an ongoing process of sanctification. We must actively address and expel any invading or trespassing demonic spirits from the soul and body so that Christ's lordship can fully extend over every part of our lives. Jesus has already provided complete provision for the healing and freedom of the whole person through His work on the cross and the power of His blood. Yet part of our responsibility is to cooperate with God's ongoing work in us. So how do demon's find their way in?

Demonic spirits find their way inside through unrepented habitual sin, life circumstances, or inheritance from generational curses. If we continually knowingly sin with no remorse or repentance, we open the door for the enemy to step in. Sometimes we go through horrible life circumstances that are traumatic and these are times evil spirits take advantage of us. And finally, demons work through the bloodline. There are certain generational curses we can see that are passed down through a family such as a spirit of poverty. Mental illness is a generational curse. A family can have a string of alcoholics from the grandfather, to the father, to the son. There are inherited diseases like high cholesterol.

When it comes to bloodlines, our blood is spiritual and there are mysteries about our blood that we will never understand. We are born in a natural world by natural parents with a natural bloodline that carried these curses that we were born into. And there's only one cure for the things you have inherited from natural blood, that's the greater blood of the Lord Jesus Christ. When you mix faith with it, you can be delivered from all curses.

Most Christians really don't need deliverance from a demon, instead they need deliverance from ignorance. There's exceptions to that, but most people simply need knowledge. They need to know the weapons that have been made available to them, and release them against the strategy of the enemy. That's what these prayers are for. They are a template for you to bring your struggles to the light. James 5:16 says, *"Confess your trespasses to one another, and pray for one another, that you may be healed."* The minute you bring it to the light, you break the power over you, because Satan works in darkness whereas God works in the light. Satan works in the lie. God works in the truth.

LEGION

"Then they came to the other side of the sea, to the country of the Gadarenes. And when He had come out of the boat, immediately there met Him out of the tombs a man with an unclean spirit, who had his dwelling among the tombs; and no one could bind him, not even with chains, because he had often been bound with shackles and chains. And the chains had been pulled apart by him, and the shackles broken in pieces; neither could anyone tame him. And always, night and day, he was in the mountains and in the tombs, crying out and cutting himself with stones. When he saw Jesus from afar, he ran and worshiped Him. And he cried out with a loud voice and said, 'What have I to do with You, Jesus, Son of the Most High God? I implore You by God that You do not torment me.' For He said to him, 'Come out of the man, unclean spirit!' Then He asked him, 'What is your name?' And he answered, saying, 'My name is **Legion***; for we are many.'"* (Mark 5:1-9)

Legion[1]

The biblical account of Legion shows a man possessed by a vast number of demons. We can infer that the man who was possessed had up to 6,000 evil spirits inside of him as a legion in the Roman army had 5,000 to 6,000 soldiers in a military unit. So collectively these demons called themselves Legion.

In many cases, demons operate in clusters or groups, banding together to dominate and control specific aspects of a person's life. At the head of each such group is typically a principal or ruling demon, the primary spirit that first gained entry into that particular area of the person's life. By being the initial intruder, this ruling demon secures a position of authority, essentially becoming the "ruler." Once established, it paves the way for additional demons to enter and reinforce control, creating a layered, cooperative oppression that makes the bondage deeper and more resistant to removal.

The Bible passage opens with Jesus and His disciples arriving by boat on the eastern side of the Sea of Galilee, in the area known as the Gadarenes. Immediately upon stepping out, they are confronted by a man possessed by an *"unclean spirit"* emerging from the tombs. Tombs were considered ritually unclean in Jewish culture.

The man was in a wretched state. He lived among the tombs, unbound by any restraints, despite repeated attempts with chains and shackles, which he supernaturally breaks. Day and night, he wanders the mountains and tombs, screaming and self-harming by cutting himself with stones. This illustrates the destructive power of demonic possession: not just physical strength beyond human norms, but also profound mental and emotional torment, leading to self-destruction and social isolation. No one could *"tame him"*, setting up a contrast with Jesus' effortless authority.

---

1. Legion (KJV, YLT, NASB, NIV, NKJV, NLT, ESV, CSB)

Spotting Jesus from a distance, *"he ran and worshipped Him."* This shows that demon possession is never under control of a person 24 hours a day. The man was able to decide for himself that he wanted deliverance. Through the man, the demons cry out loudly, addressing Jesus as *"Son of the Most High God."* They plead, *"What have I to do with You?"* (a rhetorical way of saying "Leave us alone!") and begged not to be tormented. This highlights that even evil spirits acknowledge Jesus' superiority and dread His power that we have access to.

Mark inserts a narrative aside: Jesus had already commanded the unclean spirit to *"come out of the man."* This explains the demons' plea, they are reacting to Jesus' exorcism command, which they know they cannot ultimately resist. Jesus asks the spirit's name. The response, *"My name is Legion; for we are many,"* reveals that the man is possessed not by one demon but by a multitude, an overwhelming force. This underscores the scale of the possession and amplifies the miracle's significance: Jesus overpowers not just a single entity but an entire army of demons with a word.

I Feel Isolated

Heavenly Father,

Right now my mind feels so isolated, like I'm in a fog, cut off from everyone, and even from You. The loneliness is mental as much as emotional; thoughts swirl that I'm unseen, unheard, and unimportant. It weighs on me, makes everything feel distant and gray. I don't know how to bridge this gap on my own.

Lord, thank You that Your Word says You are near to the brokenhearted and save the crushed in spirit. Thank You that even when I feel abandoned, You have promised never to leave me or forsake me. Thank You that You are my refuge and strength, a very present help in trouble, and that nothing can separate me from Your love.

Help me in this place of mental isolation. Draw near to me in a way I can feel. Quiet the racing thoughts, calm the emptiness, and let me sense Your presence. Renew my mind with Your truth. Replace lies of abandonment with the reality that You are closer than my breath. When I feel disconnected from others, remind me that You are the friend who sticks closer than a brother.

Give me strength to reach out to others and open doors for real connection. Protect my mind from spiraling deeper. Guard it with Your peace that surpasses understanding. Help me trust that this season won't last forever, and that You're working in the silence.

I cast this isolation on You because You care for me. Hold my mind steady. Let me feel seen, known, and loved by You right now.

In Jesus' name,

Amen.

My Lies Hurt Those I Love

Heavenly Father,

I confess my struggle with lying. I see how it's become a habit. Lies damage trust, hurt people, and grieve Your Spirit. I feel guilty and trapped in this pattern, and I don't want it to define me anymore.

Lord, forgive me for the lies I've told. Forgive me for choosing deception over truth, for fearing consequences more than fearing You, for letting dishonesty become my default. I repent fully.

Thank You that You are the God of truth who cannot lie. Thank You that You delight in people who are trustworthy and that You give grace to change.

Help me now, God. Put a guard over my mouth so that truth comes out naturally instead of lies. When the temptation to lie arises, give me the courage and quick conviction to stop and choose honesty instead. Replace fear of truth's cost with trust in Your protection and provision.

Root out any fear, insecurity, pride, or shame that fuels lying. Give me wisdom to speak truth in love, even when it's hard. Help me make amends where my lies have hurt others. Grant me humility to apologize and rebuild trust.

Strengthen me for the moments I feel weak. Fill me with Your Holy Spirit so that truth flows from me as naturally as breathing. Let my words reflect Your character.

Thank You for Your patience and mercy. Thank You for the fresh start every morning. I receive Your forgiveness, cleansing, and power to walk in truth right now.

In Jesus' name,

Amen.

I Swear Persistently

Heavenly Father,

I come to You today carrying the weight of my swearing and bad language. Words come out of my mouth that I regret the instant they leave. They hurt people, dishonor You, and damage my witness. I don't want my tongue to betray my heart. I want my words to reflect Your character.

Lord, forgive me for the profane words I've spoken. Forgive me for using language that grieves Your Holy Spirit and gives the enemy a foothold. I repent of all the influences that shape my speech instead of Your truth. Cleanse me completely.

Thank You that You are the God who changes hearts and tames tongues. Thank You that the same Holy Spirit who lives in me can produce self-control, gentleness, and a pure mouth. Thank You that You do not leave me stuck in old patterns, You can make all things new.

Help me now, God. Put a guard over my mouth and keep watch over the door of my lips. When habit tries to take over, give me the quick pause to choose silence or a better word. Replace filthy language with words that are helpful for building others up according to their needs.

Renew my mind so my heart produces clean speech naturally. When I slip, help me catch it immediately. Give me wisdom to avoid environments that feed this habit, and surround me with people who speak life so I can learn from them.

Thank You for Your patience with me. Thank You for grace that covers every failure and strength for every new moment. I receive Your help right now; new heart, new words, new freedom.

In Jesus' name,

Amen.

Sometimes I Turn to Self-Harm to Numb the Pain

Heavenly Father,

Sometimes I resort to self-harm. The urge to hurt myself feels so strong some-times, like it's the only way to release the pain. I hate what it does to me, the scars it leaves, the secrecy, the guilt afterward, and how it pulls me away from You and from life. I don't want to live like this anymore. I need You to rescue me.

Lord, forgive me for every time I've turned to self-harm instead of to You. Forgive me for believing lies that I deserve pain, that I'm worthless, or that this is the only relief. I repent of hurting the body You created and called good. Find me in my darkness.

Thank You that You see every hidden wound and every tear I cry alone. Thank You that Jesus took my pain on the cross so I don't have to carry it. Thank You for loving me even in this struggle.

Deliver me, God. Break the power of this urge right now in Jesus' name. When the impulse comes give me the strength to pause, cry out to You, and choose life instead. Replace the need to hurt myself with Your comfort and healthier ways to feel and release. Heal the deep wounds inside that drive this behavior.

Guard my mind from lies of self-hatred; flood it with Your truth: that I am fearfully and wonderfully made, that I am loved beyond measure, that my life has purpose and value in You. Give me courage to reach for help because You often heal through community. Protect me from danger in moments of crisis. Surround me with Your angels. I receive Your deliverance, healing, and strength right now by faith.

In Jesus' name,

Amen.

Mental Torment Causes Me to Cry Out!

Heavenly Father,

I come to You today carrying the heavy burden of watching __________ suffer with mental disorders that cause them to cry out with loud, sudden outbursts. The sounds of their distress break me. I feel helpless and overwhelmed watching someone I love so much be tormented in their mind. Lord, You see every tear, every cry, every moment of inner chaos. You hear every unspoken plea buried beneath their pain. You know exactly what is happening inside them.

Jesus, You are the Deliverer. You set the captives free. You calmed storms with a word. You cast out tormenting spirits and restored minds to peace and clarity. I ask You now, in Your mighty name, to deliver __________ from this mental torment. Break every chain, silence every voice of despair, lift every heavy cloud, and bring Your light into the darkest places of their mind. Command peace to come, peace that guards their heart and mind. Heal what is broken, restore what is lost, and give them relief.

Surround __________ with Your presence. Let them feel You holding them even when they cannot feel anything else. I stand in Your authority over any spiritual oppression and command every unclean spirit of torment to leave __________ now, in Jesus' name, and never return!

Thank You that You are near the brokenhearted and save the crushed in spirit. Thank You that no mental torment is stronger than Your power. Thank You that You hear every cry and that You are already at work, even when we cannot see it yet. I entrust __________ fully to You.

In Jesus' name,

Amen.

Deliver Me From These Demons!

Heavenly Father,

I come to You now in desperate need. I am oppressed, bound, and afflicted by forces far beyond my own strength. But You came to set the captive free. You have authority over every power of darkness. You are greater than any legion. You are the One who the demons fear and obey and give us the Word to operate under Your authority.

In Your mighty name, Jesus, I renounce and reject every unclean spirit, every demonic force, every stronghold, every assignment of darkness that has bound me! I refuse their lies, their accusations, their control. I break every chain, every yoke, every legal ground they claim over my life. Whether through sin, generational patterns, trauma, curses, or any entry point known or unknown.

I command you, in the name of Jesus: Come out! Come out of me now! Every spirit, every power, every torment; leave my body, my mind, and soul! Go to the place appointed for you by the Lord Jesus Christ. You have no right here. The blood of Jesus speaks against you. The cross has disarmed you. You must obey.

Lord Jesus, fill the void they leave. Cast out every unclean spirit and replace it with Your Holy Spirit. Clothe me in Your righteousness and restore me to my right mind. Heal every wound they have inflicted. Let Your light drive out every shadow. I declare Your victory over me: No weapon formed against me shall prosper. Greater is He who is in me than he who is in the world.

Thank You Jesus, for coming to this "tomb" of my life. I receive Your deliverance now, complete, permanent, sealed by Your blood.

In Jesus' name,

Amen.

UNCLEAN SPIRIT

*"Now there was a man in their synagogue with an **unclean spirit**. And he cried out, saying, 'Let us alone! What have we to do with You, Jesus of Nazareth? Did You come to destroy us? I know who You are—the Holy One of God!' But Jesus rebuked him, saying, 'Be quiet, and come out of him!' And when the **unclean spirit** had convulsed him and cried out with a loud voice, he came out of him. Then they were all amazed, so that they questioned among themselves, saying, 'What is this? What new doctrine is this? For with authority He commands even the unclean spirits, and they obey Him.'"* (Mark 1:23-27)

Unclean Spirit[1]

An unclean spirit in the New Testament of the Bible is a term used to describe a demon or evil spirit that can possess or oppress a person, causing torment, abnormal behavior, or spiritual affliction. The word "unclean" emphasizes their moral and spiritual opposition to God's holiness and purity, contrasting with the Holy Spirit. These beings are understood to be under the authority of Satan, capable of entering and controlling human beings until they are cast out by divine power.

Mark chapter 1 is part of the Gospel of Mark's account of Jesus' early ministry in Galilee, specifically in the town of Capernaum. This passage immediately follows Jesus' teaching in the synagogue (verses 21–22), where the people are already astonished by His authoritative teaching. The event described here is one of the first miracles recorded in Mark, an exorcism, that demonstrates Jesus' power over demonic forces.

> *"Now there was a man in their synagogue with an **unclean spirit**. And he cried out,"*

The scene is in a Jewish synagogue on the Sabbath, a place of worship and teaching. A man enters who is possessed by an unclean spirit. The man's condition isn't described in detail, but possession typically manifests in abnormal behavior or speech. The spirit, speaking through the man, interrupts Jesus' teaching. This *"crying out"* shows the spirit's agitation in Jesus' presence.

---

1. Evil Spirt (NLT)
   Impure Spirit (NIV)
   Unclean Spirit (KJV, YLT, NASB, NKJV, ESV, CSB)

"saying, 'Let us alone! What have we to do with You, Jesus of Nazareth? Did You come to destroy us? I know who You are—the Holy One of God!'"

The unclean spirit addresses Jesus directly, using *"us"* (possibly referring to itself and other demons). It pleads to be left alone and questions Jesus' purpose. The spirit confesses Jesus as *"the Holy One of God."* Ironically, while human observers are just beginning to recognize Jesus' authority, the demonic world already knows His true nature. This verse highlights a recurring motif in Mark: supernatural beings acknowledge Jesus' identity before humans do.

"But Jesus rebuked him, saying, 'Be quiet, and come out of him!'"

Jesus *"rebukes"* the spirit, ordering silence and expulsion. Unlike contemporary Jewish exorcists who used rituals, incantations, or objects, Jesus casts out the demon with a simple, authoritative word. The command to *"be quiet"* prevents the spirit from further speech, possibly to avoid unwanted publicity or to control the timing of revelations about His identity.

*"And when the **unclean spirit** had convulsed him and cried out with a loud voice, he came out of him."*

The spirit obeys but not without resistance. It convulses the man and lets out a final loud cry. This physical manifestation shows the reality of the possession and the power struggle, but the spirit ultimately exits, leaving the man unharmed.

"Then they were all amazed, so that they questioned among themselves, saying, 'What is this? What new doctrine is this? For with authority He commands even the unclean spirits, and they obey Him.'"

The synagogue audience is *"amazed"* leading to discussion. They describe Jesus' teaching as *"new doctrine"* because it's accompanied by undeniable power even over unclean spirits. Unlike the scribes who taught based on tradition or rabbis' interpretations, Jesus' words carry inherent power that effects change in the spiritual and physical realms.

An unclean spirit is remarkably broad, encompassing a wide array of demonic influences that can oppress or afflict individuals. If you have endured hardships in your life, whether through trauma, sin, or inherited burdens, you may have unknowingly opened doors to unclean spirits at some point, allowing their influence to linger in areas of brokenness. Yet, true healing is always available, for no wound is beyond the reach of God's grace. Use the prayers in this section to guide you through the process of repentance, renunciation, and restoration, inviting the healing that only Jesus can bring, freeing you to walk in His light and wholeness.

I Have Unresolved Childhood Trauma

Heavenly Father,

I come to You today carrying the weight of trauma from my childhood. The child inside me still hurts, still feels unsafe, still carries shame or anger or numbness that I don't always understand. These memories and feelings surface unexpectedly, and they affect how I see myself. I don't want this to define me anymore.

Lord, You saw every moment, I don't have to hide it from You. Thank You that You were there, even when I felt alone. Thank You that Jesus understands deep suffering so He could heal mine. Thank You that You are close to the brokenhearted and save the crushed in spirit.

I ask You now to help me work through this trauma. Bring Your light into the dark places of my memory and heart. Gently uncover what needs healing. Replace the lies that trauma planted with Your truth: that I'm fearfully and wonderfully made, chosen and loved, and that You are my safe refuge.

Heal the wounds in my soul, body, and mind. Calm the triggers, soften the shame, release the anger or fear that's been stored up. Give me peace to guard my heart and thoughts. Help me forgive where needed, not to excuse harm, but to free myself from bitterness. Strengthen me to process this with grace.

Restore what was stolen. Make beauty from these ashes. Let this pain become a testimony of Your redeeming power.

Thank You for beginning this work in me and for promising to complete it. I receive Your comfort, Your strength, and Your healing today. Hold the child in me close.

In Jesus' name,

Amen.

The Abuse I Experienced Still Lingers

Heavenly Father,

I come to You today carrying the deep pain of abuse from someone who was supposed to be close, safe, and loving. That betrayal wounded me in ways that still hurt. My heart aches, and I struggle to feel whole.

Lord, You saw every moment. You were there when no one else was, and You wept with me. Thank You that You hate what was done to me. Thank You that Jesus bore my griefs and carried my sorrows so I don't have to carry them alone.

I ask You now to heal me from this abuse. Bring Your gentle light into the darkest places of my heart and memories. Expose lies the abuse planted and replace them with Your truth: that I am fearfully and wonderfully made, chosen and dearly loved, and that You are my safe refuge.

Heal my body where it remembers pain, my mind where triggers steal peace, my emotions where trust feels impossible, and my spirit where shame lingers. Calm the storms inside me. Help me grieve what was lost and comfort me as only You can. Restore what was broken or stolen: my joy, my confidence, healthy relationships, a sense of worth.

Part of this journey is forgiveness so please give me grace. I am ready to forgive, please release the poison of bitterness so I can be free. Lead me to safe help who can walk with me, because You often heal through community.

Hold me close today, Father. Remind me moment by moment that I am seen, known, and fiercely loved by You. Thank You for beginning this healing and for promising to complete it. I receive Your comfort, strength, and hope right now.

In Jesus' name,

Amen.

Set Me Free From Addiction

Heavenly Father,

I come to You today broken, weary, and desperate. This addiction has taken hold of me and it has become a chain around my life. It steals my peace, damages my body, hurts the people I love, and pulls me away from You. I hate what it has done to me, and I hate that I keep returning to it even when I promise myself I won't.

Lord, I confess this addiction as sin and bondage. I repent for every time I have turned to this instead of to You, for every lie I've believed that says I need this to cope. Forgive me completely. Wash me clean by the blood of Jesus.

Right now, in the mighty name of Jesus Christ, I renounce and break every chain of this addiction. I break every stronghold, every craving, every mental obsession, every emotional trigger, every physical dependence, every generational pattern, every demonic influence that has kept me bound. I command every unclean spirit connected to this addiction to leave me now and never return! You have no legal right here! The blood of Jesus has purchased me completely.

Deliver me, God. Break the power of this compulsion. Replace cravings with Your presence. Fill the empty places with Your Holy Spirit. Renew my mind. Heal the wounds that first opened the door to this addiction. Restore what has been stolen. Protect me from relapse and surround me with people who will walk with me.

Thank You for the cross that covers every failure and the empty tomb that proves Your power to resurrect even the most broken life. I receive Your deliverance, Your strength, and Your freedom right now by faith. From this day forward, I choose to live free in You.

In Jesus' name,

Amen.

This Anger Wells Up Inside Me

Heavenly Father,

I come to You right now with my anger laid bare. It rises up so fast. It burns in my chest, spills out in words I regret, actions I hate, and leaves me ashamed and exhausted afterward. I don't want to live like this anymore. I don't want anger to define me or damage the people I love or my walk with You.

Lord, forgive me for every time my anger has turned to sin and poisons my heart. I repent of letting it rule me instead of Your Spirit. Search my heart and show me the roots. Bring them into Your light and heal them.

Thank You that You do not leave me stuck in this. Thank You that Jesus understands righteous anger and also models perfect self-control. Thank You that You have not given me a spirit of fear or rage. Thank You that Your Spirit produces patience, kindness, gentleness, and self-control in me.

Help me now, God. When anger starts to rise, give me the pause to breathe and choose Your way instead. Teach me to be quick to listen, slow to speak, and slow to become angry. Replace my quick temper with Your peace. Give me grace to forgive as You've forgiven me.

Renew my mind. Help me see people and situations through Your eyes, not through the lens of offense or threat. Give me wisdom to set healthy boundaries without rage, to speak truth in love, and to walk away when needed. Protect my relationships from the fallout of my anger; restore where damage has been done.

Thank You for loving me and Your patience with me. I receive Your help right now.

In Jesus' name,

Amen.

My Mind is Filled With Impure Sexual Thoughts

Heavenly Father,

I come to You right now with my heart exposed, confessing the battle I face with unclean thoughts, lust, sexual fantasies, pornography, or any form of impurity that keeps pulling at my mind and body. These thoughts and desires rise up uninvited and leave me feeling guilty and distant from You. I hate how they dishonor You and harm me, yet I keep returning to them. I need Your rescue.

Lord, forgive me completely for every impure thought, look, action, or indulgence. I repent of letting lust rule my mind and heart instead of Your Spirit. Forgive me for any idolatry of pleasure, for objectifying others, for feeding these desires instead of fleeing them.

Thank You that Jesus understands temptation yet never sinned, and that You provide a way out of every temptation. Thank You that You have not given me a spirit of lust or bondage, but of power, love, and a sound mind.

Help me now, God. Take every unclean, lustful thought captive and make it obedient to Christ. When temptation comes, give me the grace to flee immediately. Guard my eyes, my mind, my heart, and my body. Break any strongholds, addictions, or generational patterns tied to this area.

When I fall, strengthen me to pursue self-control. Let my life honor You in my thoughts and actions.

Thank You for Your mercy that is new every morning. Thank You for the freedom and joy that come from walking in purity. I receive Your help, cleansing, and deliverance right now by faith.

In Jesus' name,

Amen.

Break This Generational Curse of Poverty

Heavenly Father,

My family has been trapped in a cycle of poverty for generations and I don't want this pattern to repeat with me. I see how this has affected my parents, and my grandparents, and I refuse to let it continue in my life or in the lives of my children.

Lord, I confess any ways sin, disobedience, unbelief, or ungodly agreements (known or unknown) have opened the door to this curse. If there has been idolatry of money, fear of lack, dishonesty, laziness, generational unbelief, or any other root, I repent on behalf of myself and my family line.

Today I renounce and break every generational curse of poverty, lack, debt, limitation, and scarcity over my family line. I declare that Christ has redeemed us from the curse of the law, and no curse can stand against His finished work. I cancel every assignment of the enemy to keep my family in financial bondage.

Father, I claim Your promise to bless those who love and obey You to a thousand generations. Pour out Your blessing on my household. Restore the years we have lacked.

Replace fear of lack with faith in Your provision. Teach me to be a wise, generous steward of whatever You entrust to me. Give me favor in work, business, investments, and decisions. Open supernatural doors no man can shut.

I thank You in advance for the breakthrough. You hear the cry of the poor, and You delight to bless Your children. I receive Your deliverance, provision, and generational blessing right now by faith. Let this cycle end with me, and let blessing begin flowing through my family line for generations to come.

In Jesus' name,

Amen.

Mental Health Struggles End With Me

Heavenly Father,

I come before You, standing in the gap for my family line. A curse of mental health struggles has plagued us for generations. I see the pain and cycles of suffering, and I will not accept this for myself. I will not confess mental illness or torment over my life, my mind, my children, or my descendants. This ends here, in Jesus' name.

Lord, I repent, for myself and on behalf of my ancestors, for any sin, trauma, idolatry, unforgiveness, occult involvement, or ungodly agreements that opened doors to this curse. Wash us with the blood of Jesus. I renounce and break every generational curse of mental affliction, emotional torment, mind-binding spirits, instability, fear, depression, anxiety, and any related bondage operating in my family line. No curse has legal right over me or my family anymore!

I reject every spirit that has traveled through generations. I command them to leave my mind, my emotions, my DNA, my family line, and never return, in the name of Jesus. I break every chain, every legal ground, every spoken or unspoken word that has enforced this curse. It is null and void.

Father, I claim Your blessing instead. I declare soundness of mind, peace, clarity, joy, and emotional wholeness over my life and my lineage. Renew our minds, heal every wounded place, restore what trauma and darkness stole, and fill us with Your perfect peace that guards hearts and minds. Bring supernatural healing.

Thank You, Lord, that You hear the cry of the afflicted. Thank You for the blood of Jesus that speaks better things. I receive Your deliverance, renewal, and complete mental wholeness right now by faith.

In Jesus' name,

Amen.

I Have Authority Over Unclean Spirits

Heavenly Father,

I come before You in the mighty name of Jesus Christ who has all authority in heaven and on earth. I thank You that through His death, resurrection, and ascension, You have given me authority over all the power of the enemy. I thank You that the same Spirit who raised Jesus from the dead lives in me, and that greater is He who is in me than he who is in the world.

Right now, I declare and proclaim: I have been given authority in the name of Jesus Christ to trample on serpents and scorpions, and over all the power of the enemy, and nothing shall by any means hurt me. I declare that no unclean spirit has any right, legal claim, or foothold in my life, my body, my mind, my family, my home, or my future. I renounce and cancel every assignment, curse, oppression, torment, or influence of unclean spirits over me or those connected to me.

I command every unclean spirit, every demon, or any other foul spirit: **Come out now! Leave this place! Go to the feet of Jesus Christ and submit to His judgment!** You have no authority here. The blood of Jesus speaks against you. The cross has disarmed you. You must obey the name above every name: Jesus Christ!

Thank You, Father, that I am seated with Christ in heavenly places, far above all rule and authority and power and dominion. Thank You that no weapon formed against me shall prosper. Thank You that whom the Son sets free is free indeed.

I stand firm in this authority today, tomorrow, and every day forward. All glory, honor, and power belong to Jesus Christ forever.

In Jesus' name,

Amen.

Spirit of Infirmity

*"And behold, there was a woman who had a **spirit of infirmity** eighteen years, and was bent over and could in no way raise herself up. But when Jesus saw her, He called her to Him and said to her, 'Woman, you are loosed from your infirmity.' And He laid His hands on her, and immediately she was made straight, and glorified God.*

But the ruler of the synagogue answered with indignation, because Jesus had healed on the Sabbath; and he said to the crowd, 'There are six days on which men ought to work; therefore come and be healed on them, and not on the Sabbath day.'

*The Lord then answered him and said, 'Hypocrite! Does not each one of you on the Sabbath loose his ox or donkey from the stall, and lead it away to water it? So ought not this woman, being a daughter of Abraham, **whom Satan has bound**—think of it—for eighteen years, be loosed from this bond on the Sabbath?'"* (Luke 13:11-16)

Spirit of Infirmity[1]

A spirit of infirmity is an unclean spirit that inflicts prolonged physical weakness, disability, or affliction upon a person. In this verse Jesus identifies it as a form of satanic oppression, stating that Satan had *"bound"* her, highlighting its supernatural origin rather than a natural illness.

"And behold, there was a woman who had a spirit of infirmity eighteen years, and was bent over and could in no way raise herself up."

In the verse, Jesus is teaching in a synagogue on the Sabbath, the day of rest mandated in the Old Testament. A woman appears who has suffered from a debilitating condition for 18 years. The term *"spirit of infirmity"* suggests not just a natural illness but a spiritual oppression or demonic influence affecting her physically. She is hunched over and unable to straighten herself, symbolizing bondage or affliction.

"But when Jesus saw her, He called her to Him and said to her, 'Woman, you are loosed from your infirmity.'"

Jesus initiates the healing without being asked, showing His compassion and awareness of human suffering. He addresses her as *"Woman,"* a respectful term, and declares her *"loosed"* (implying release from chains or bondage).

---

1. Crippled by a spirit (NIV, NLT)
   Disabled by a spirit (CSB)
   Disabling Spirit (ESV)
   Spirit of Infirmity (KJV, YLT, NKJV)
   Sickness caused by a spirit (NASB)

By laying hands on her, she is instantly restored to full health. Her immediate response is to glorify God, underscoring that true miracles lead to worship and acknowledgment of God's work. This act demonstrates Jesus' authority over both physical diseases and spiritual entities, fulfilling His mission to *"proclaim liberty to the captives"* (Luke 4:18, quoting Isaiah 61:1).

"But the ruler of the synagogue answered with indignation, because Jesus had healed on the Sabbath; and he said to the crowd, 'There are six days on which men ought to work; therefore come and be healed on them, and not on the Sabbath day.'"

The synagogue ruler, a lay leader responsible for services, reacts with anger. His objection stems from Jewish traditions that expanded the Sabbath commandment to prohibit 39 categories of "work", including healing, which some rabbis viewed as labor. He addresses the crowd indirectly, avoiding confronting Jesus directly, which highlights his cowardice or passive-aggressiveness. This reflects a broader tension in the Gospels between Jesus and religious leaders who prioritized ritual observance over mercy. The ruler's stance misses the Sabbath's original purpose: rest, restoration, and reflection on God's deliverance.

"The Lord then answered him and said, 'Hypocrite! Does not each one of you on the Sabbath loose his ox or donkey from the stall, and lead it away to water it?'"

Jesus calls out the hypocrisy directly. He uses a common-sense analogy: Even strict observers allow untying (loosing) animals on the Sabbath for basic needs like water, as permitted in Jewish law.

> *"'So ought not this woman, being a daughter of Abraham, whom* ***Satan has bound****—think of it—for eighteen years, be loosed from this bond on the Sabbath?'"*

If animals can be *"loosed"* for compassion, how much more should a human—a *"daughter of Abraham"* (emphasizing her covenant status as part of God's chosen people)—be freed from Satan's bondage? Jesus explicitly identifies the cause as Satanic, reinforcing the spiritual dimension. The repeated use of *"loose"* ties the analogy together, arguing that healing is an act of liberation fitting for the Sabbath, which commemorates freedom from slavery in Egypt. This rebuttal exposes legalism as inconsistent and unloving, prioritizing rules over people.

Not all illnesses in the Bible are attributed to demonic causes, as Jesus healed many people with natural ailments. However, in this case, the spirit is explicitly tied to a long-term, crippling condition, suggesting demonic oppression. The passage does not provide specific details about what led to the woman being afflicted by this spirit. Rather, the Bible focuses on the power of God to overcome them. The first thing you need to pray for is for God to reveal if your infirmity is demonic or natural. From there you can go down the path of casting out the demon or prayer for supernatural healing.

Reveal the Cause of My Infirmity

Heavenly Father,

I come to You today with a heavy heart, carrying this infirmity that has afflicted me for so long. You know every detail, the pain, the limitation, the confusion, the fear it brings. I don't understand why this has happened or what is behind it, and that uncertainty weighs on me. But You are the God who sees all things, who searches hearts and minds, who gives wisdom generously without finding fault, and who exposes every hidden thing to light.

Lord, I ask You to reveal the cause of this infirmity. Show me clearly whether it is natural or whether it is demonic and needs to be confronted in Your name. Give me discernment of spirits so I can test everything and hold to what is good. Open my eyes spiritually and practically so I know exactly how to proceed in prayer and action.

Forgive me if any sin, unbelief, unforgiveness, or open door in my life has allowed this infirmity to take hold. I repent and ask for Your cleansing blood to cover me. Strengthen my faith as I wait for Your revelation. Give me peace that surpasses understanding and endurance to stand firm. Let this revelation lead to full deliverance, healing, and a testimony of Your power.

Thank You that You hear my cry and that nothing is too hard for You. Thank You for being the Revealer of mysteries and the Healer of all. I receive Your wisdom, Your guidance, and Your deliverance right now by faith.

In Jesus' name,

Amen.

Relieve Me From Arthritis

Heavenly Father,

Your Word says that Jesus Himself took my infirmities and bore my sicknesses, and by His stripes I am healed. Arthritis has caused pain, stiffness, swelling, and limitation in my body, and I refuse to accept it as permanent or inevitable. I will not let this condition define me or rob me of the life You promise in abundance.

Lord, I confess any ways sin, unforgiveness, generational patterns, or unbelief may have opened a door to affliction. I repent of these sins.

In the authority of Jesus' name, I speak directly to this arthritis: I command every spirit of infirmity, inflammation, pain, degeneration, and limitation connected to this condition to leave my body right now! Go in Jesus' name! I cast you out and forbid you to return. Every joint, every cartilage, every nerve, every cell, be restored and made whole by the power of the Holy Spirit.

Father, I declare Your promises over my body: You forgive all my sins and heal all my diseases. You are the God who heals me. I stand on the finished work of the cross, Jesus paid the price for my healing. I receive divine health, mobility, strength, and freedom from pain.

Give me wisdom for practical care so I steward this body as Your temple. Surround me with Your peace that surpasses understanding, and let this trial become a testimony of Your power.

Thank You, Lord, that You hear the cry of the afflicted. Thank You for the authority You've given me in Christ to resist the enemy and for the healing already provided in Jesus. I receive my healing by faith today: body, mind, and spirit.

In Jesus' name,

Amen.

I Have Dealt With Chronic Pain for Too Long

Heavenly Father,

I come to You today longing for relief from this chronic pain. It grips me everyday, exhausting every part of my body. It steals my sleep, my strength, my joy, my ability to live fully, and sometimes even my hope. I feel trapped in this suffering, and I cry out to You because You are the only One who can truly deliver me.

Lord Jesus, You are the Great Physician. You bore my pain and carried my sicknesses on the cross. You touched the sick, the lame, the suffering, and they were made whole. I believe You are still the same yesterday, today, and forever. I believe You can and want to set me free from this relentless pain.

In Your name, I ask You to deliver me completely from this chronic pain. Touch every inflamed joint, damaged nerve, inflamed tissue, every misfiring signal in my body. Shut down the pain pathways. Restore what is broken. Calm every storm of discomfort. Let Your healing power flow through me like rivers of living water, bringing relief, mobility, strength, and peace where there has been only torment.

I speak to this pain in Your authority: Leave my body now! You have no right to stay. I command every root of this pain to be uprooted and cast out. My body is the temple of the Holy Spirit, and it belongs to Jesus Christ. Pain, you must bow to His name!

Thank You for the promise that You will restore the years the locusts have eaten. I thank You in advance for the day I wake up without this pain for the freedom to move without this constant burden. I receive Your healing touch, Your strength, and Your peace right now by faith.

In Jesus' name,

Amen.

This Disability Will Not Define Me Anymore

Heavenly Father,

I come to You today carrying the weight of this disability that has shaped so much of my life. It limits my body and sometimes makes me feel less than whole. I have lived with it for so long, but I refuse to accept that this is my permanent portion. I believe You are the God who heals and delivers from every affliction.

Lord Jesus, You touched the paralyzed man and said, *"Rise, take up your mat and walk,"* and he did. You healed the woman bent over for eighteen years with a word. You gave hearing to the deaf, speech to the mute, and wholeness to the disabled. Your power and compassion has never diminished.

I ask You now, to deliver me from this disability. Heal every part of my body that is affected. Restore function where it has been lost. Renew systems that have been damaged or never fully formed. Let Your healing flow through me, reversing what has been broken, and bringing full mobility, strength, and freedom.

I speak to this disability in Your authority: Leave my body now! You have no right to stay. The blood of Jesus has defeated every curse of infirmity. I command every root of this condition to be cast out. My body is the temple of the Holy Spirit, and it belongs to Jesus Christ. Disability, you must bow to His name!

Thank You, Father, that You see every limitation I live with. Thank You that You are near the afflicted and save those who cry out to You. Thank You that You are already at work in my body, even when I cannot yet feel it. I thank You in advance for the day I move freely. I receive Your healing power, Your strength, and Your deliverance right now by faith.

In Jesus' name,

Amen.

I Will Not Inherit Any Disease Passed Through My Family

Heavenly Father,

I come before Your throne as my Healer. I stand in the gap for my family line, acknowledging that a curse of ______________ has plagued us across generations. It has brought so much suffering, and I refuse to let it continue. I will not accept this as my inheritance. I will not confess sickness, cancer, or early death over my life, my body, my children, or my descendants. This stops here, in Jesus' name.

Lord, I repent for any sin, iniquity, unbelief, idolatry, fear, or ungodly agreements (known or unknown) that may have opened the door to this curse. Forgive us completely. Wash us with the blood of Jesus. I renounce and break every generational curse of sickness, disease, infirmity, cancer, and premature death operating in my bloodline. No curse has legal right over me or my family anymore.

I reject every spirit of infirmity, every assignment of sickness, every hereditary pattern of this illness. I command them to leave my body, my DNA, my family line, and never return, in the name of Jesus. I break every chain, every legal ground, every word that has enforced this curse. It is null and void.

Father, I claim Your blessing instead. I declare divine health over my body and my family. By Jesus' stripes we are healed. You are the God who forgives all our sins and heals all our diseases. Let this be the generation where the curse ends and blessing begins.

Thank You, Lord, that You hear the cry of the afflicted. Thank You for the blood that speaks better things. I receive Your deliverance and complete healing right now by faith. This sickness will not continue in my line.

In Jesus' name,

Amen.

My Loved One is Suffering From Cognitive Decline

Heavenly Father,

I come before You today aching for ___________. The cognitive decline they are experiencing breaks me. I see them struggle in their own mind, and it feels like a slow theft of who they are. Lord, You know every detail of this pain. You love ___________ even more than I do, and nothing is hidden from You.

Jesus, You are the Restorer of minds and the Healer of every affliction. You gave clarity to those who were confused, restored memory and understanding, and demonstrated Your authority over every form of sickness. I believe You are still the same today. I believe You can reverse what medicine calls irreversible.

In Your mighty name, deliver ___________ from this cognitive decline. Restore their mind completely. Renew every neuron, every pathway, every memory center that has been damaged or lost. Bring back clarity where there is confusion. Let forgotten names, faces, stories, and joys return vividly.

I speak to this condition in Your authority: Cognitive decline, leave ___________'s mind and body now! Every spirit of confusion be halted and reversed! You have no right to steal what God created. The blood of Jesus has defeated every curse of infirmity. I command healing virtue to flow through ___________'s brain right now.

Thank You Lord that You carry ___________ when we cannot. Thank You for the promise of a day when their mind will be made new, every tear wiped away, and every memory restored in Your presence forever.

Let Your love be felt in every moment. I entrust them completely to You, trusting You are already at work.

In Jesus' name,

Amen.

Help Me Overcome an Eating Disorder

Heavenly Father,

I come to You today desperate for freedom from this eating disorder that has taken over my life. It has stolen my peace, damaged my body, twisted my thoughts, and made me feel distant from the people I love. I hate what it has done to me, and I hate that I keep returning to it even when I promise myself I won't. I am powerless on my own.

Lord, I confess this eating disorder as sin and bondage. I repent for every time I've turned to food, restriction, or body control. I repent for believing lies that my worth is tied to my size or appearance. I repent for harming the body You created and called good. Forgive me completely. Wash me clean by the blood of Jesus.

In the name of Jesus Christ, I renounce and break every chain of this eating disorder. I break every stronghold of control, perfectionism, self-hatred, shame, fear, trauma, comparison, and deception that has kept me bound. I command every tormenting spirit connected to this addiction to leave me now and never return! You have no legal right here. The blood of Jesus has purchased me completely.

Deliver me, God. Break the power of every obsessive thought, every lie that says I need this to feel okay. Fill the places this disorder has controlled with Your peace. Restore a healthy relationship with food and with my body. Renew my mind so I see myself as fearfully and wonderfully made.

Thank You for Your relentless love that never gives up on me. I receive Your deliverance, Your healing, and Your freedom right now by faith. From this day forward, I choose to live free in You.

In Jesus' name,

Amen.

I Am Loosed From This Sickness

Heavenly Father,

I come before You in the name of Jesus who has all authority over sickness. You are the God who heals every disease and who sent Jesus to proclaim deliverance to the captives. I thank You that the same power that raised Jesus from the dead lives in me right now.

Lord, I acknowledge that some sickness in my body may be rooted in a spirit of infirmity. I refuse to accept this as my permanent portion. I refuse to let any spirit of infirmity have legal right or foothold in my life any longer.

In the name of Jesus Christ, I renounce and reject every spirit of infirmity operating in my body, my mind, or my life! Whether it came through generational patterns, trauma, curses, sin, or any other entry point. I break every chain, every yoke, every assignment, and every legal claim these spirits have held over me.

I command you, spirit of infirmity and sickness: Come out of me now! Leave my body and every part of me! Go to the feet of Jesus Christ and submit to His judgment! You have no authority here. The blood of Jesus has defeated you. The cross has disarmed you. You must obey His name over every other!

Lord Jesus, flood my body with Your healing virtue. Restore my body to perfect order as You originally designed it. Let Your resurrection life flow through me now.

Thank You, Father, that You are near the afflicted and save those who cry out to You. Thank You for the cross that paid for my complete deliverance. I receive my healing and freedom right now by faith.

In Jesus' name,

Amen.

DEAF AND DUMB SPIRIT

*"Then one of the crowd answered and said, 'Teacher, I brought You my son, who has a mute spirit. And wherever it seizes him, it throws him down; he foams at the mouth, gnashes his teeth, and becomes rigid.' Then they brought him to Him. And when he saw Him, immediately the spirit convulsed him, and he fell on the ground and wallowed, foaming at the mouth. So He asked his father, 'How long has this been happening to him?' And he said, 'From childhood. And often he has thrown him both into the fire and into the water to destroy him. But if You can do anything, have compassion on us and help us.' Jesus said to him, 'If you can believe, all things are possible to him who believes.' Immediately the father of the child cried out and said with tears, 'Lord, I believe; help my unbelief!' He rebuked the unclean spirit, saying to it, **Deaf and dumb spirit**, I command you, come out of him and enter him no more!' Then the spirit cried out, convulsed him greatly, and came out of him. And he became as one dead, so that many said, 'He is dead.' But Jesus took him by the hand and lifted him up, and he arose."* (Mark 9:17-27)

Deaf and Dumb Spirit[1]

A deaf and dumb spirit is an example of how unclean spirits can afflict us physically. This type of spirit is seen as a "strong man" demon that may contribute to other conditions like blindness, insanity, or accident-prone behavior.

In this passage from Mark, a man approaches Jesus explaining that he brought his son, who is tormented by a *"mute spirit."* The demon's effect on the boy rendered him speechless. The spirit also caused violent seizures: it seizes him, throws him down, leads to foaming at the mouth, teeth gnashing, and rigidity which are symptoms resembling epilepsy.

Jesus instructs the disciples to bring the boy to Him. As the boy is brought forward, the spirit reacts violently to Jesus' presence, convulsing him and causing him to fall, wallow, and foam at the mouth, demonstrating the demon's awareness of Jesus' threat and its attempt to harm the boy further. Jesus inquires about the duration, and the father reveals it began in childhood, with the spirit often trying to kill the boy by throwing him into fire or water.

Jesus responds by emphasizing faith: *"If you can believe, all things are possible to him who believes."* This isn't a blanket promise for any desire but highlights that faith in God unlocks divine intervention in seemingly impossible situations. The father's immediate, tearful response, *"Lord, I believe; help my unbelief!"* is a raw confession of partial faith. This verse is often cited as a model for honest prayer amid doubt.

Seeing the growing crowd, Jesus acts swiftly to prevent sensationalism. He rebukes the *"deaf and dumb spirit"* (expanding on the father's *"mute"* description to include deafness), commanding it to leave and never return. The spirit's exit is

---

1. Deaf and Mute Spirit (NASB, NIV, ESV, CSB)
   Dumb and Deaf Spirit (KJV, YLT, NKJV)
   Spirit that makes this boy unable to hear and speak (NLT)

dramatic: it cries out, convulses the boy intensely, and leaves him appearing dead, prompting onlookers to declare him so. Jesus then takes the boy's hand, lifts him up, and he arises.

This passage illustrates Jesus' supreme authority over evil spirits that is available to His followers as well. It emphasizes the role of faith: not perfect or unwavering, but sincere and reliant on God, as seen in the father's plea. Theologically, it shows demonic possession as a real force causing physical and spiritual torment in the New Testament era, with Jesus as the ultimate deliverer. It also serves as a rebuke to unbelief and a call to deeper dependence on God through prayer.

I Want to Hear Creation's Song

Heavenly Father,

I come to You today with a longing I have carried since childhood. I have never heard a bird sing, a loved one's laugh, music, the sound of rain, or even my own voice clearly. I have adapted, I have learned to communicate in my own ways, but there is still a deep ache inside me to hear, to experience the world of sound that others take for granted.

Lord, I have full confidence that You are the God who opens ears, restores hearing, and makes the deaf hear. In the Gospels, Jesus touched the deaf, spoke to their condition, and said *"Be opened!"*—and they heard (Mark 7:34-35). Lord Jesus, I believe there is a deaf spirit that has bound my ears and kept me from hearing. I refuse to let any spirit of deafness have legal right or hold over my life anymore.

In the name and authority of Jesus Christ, I renounce and reject this deaf spirit operating in my body, my ears, my auditory nerves, my brain, or any part of me. I break every chain, every yoke, every assignment, and every legal claim these spirits have held over my hearing.

I command you, deaf spirit, **Come out of me now!** You have no authority here! The blood of Jesus has defeated you. The cross has disarmed you. You must obey the name above every name, Jesus Christ!

Thank You, Father, for the power that is already at work in my body. I receive my hearing right now by faith. I thank You now for the moment I hear clearly, for the testimony this will become, and for the glory that will go to Your name alone.

In Jesus' name,

Amen.

Help Me Communicate With My Loved Ones

Heavenly Father,

You are the God who looses the tongues of the mute, who opens silent mouths, who commands speech where there was none. You are the same Jesus who touched the speechless and commanded their tongues to work, who gave voice where there was silence, who made the impossible possible with a word.

Lord Jesus, You still have that same authority today. You still release locked tongues. You still open silent mouths. I believe this is Your desire for me. I believe You want me to speak, to praise You with my own voice, to declare Your works, to talk with my family and friends, to sing, to laugh, to proclaim Your name. I refuse to let any spirit of muteness have legal right or hold over my voice, my throat, my mind, or my life.

In the name and authority of Jesus Christ, I renounce and reject every dumb spirit, every mute spirit, every spirit of silence or speechlessness operating in my body, my throat, my vocal cords, my tongue, my mouth, my brain, or any part of me. I break every chain, every yoke, every assignment, and every legal claim these spirits have held over my ability to speak.

I command you, dumb spirit, **Come out of me now!** You have no authority here! The blood of Jesus has defeated you. The cross has disarmed you. You must obey the name above every name, Jesus Christ!

Thank You, Father, because I know You hear me. I receive my speech right now by faith. I thank You for the moment I will speak my first clear word and for the testimony this healing will become. My voice belongs to Jesus Christ alone.

In Jesus' name,

Amen.

I See You With My Heart but Not With My Eyes

Heavenly Father,

I come before You, the One who has all authority over every spirit and every form of darkness. You are the God who opens blind eyes, who gives sight to those born blind, who touches the blind man with mud and tells him to wash in the pool of Siloam, and he comes back seeing. Your power has never changed.

Lord Jesus, I believe a spirit of blindness has bound my eyes and kept me from seeing. I refuse to let any spirit of blindness or visual infirmity have legal right or hold over my vision, my eyes, my optic nerves, my brain, or any part of me.

In the name and authority of Jesus Christ, I renounce and reject every spirit of blindness, every spirit of darkness or sightlessness operating in my body. I break every chain, every yoke, every assignment, and every legal claim these spirits have held over my ability to see.

I command you, spirit of blindness **Come out of me now! Leave my eyes!** You have no authority here! The blood of Jesus has defeated you. The cross has disarmed you. You must obey the name above every name, Jesus Christ!

Lord Jesus, I ask You to touch my eyes as You touched the blind. Open them now! Let light flood in clearly, colors appear vividly, shapes and faces become sharp and beautiful. Let me see the world You created with perfect clarity.

Thank You, Father, for the power that is already at work in my eyes. I receive my sight right now by faith. I thank You in advance for the first thing I will see when my eyes open, for the day I look at Your creation and praise You with my own vision, for the testimony this will become.

In Jesus' name,

Amen.

I Will Live Seizure Free

Heavenly Father,

I come to You today believing You are the God who stops seizures, calms electrical storms in the brain, and restores perfect order to every nerve and cell. You are the same Jesus who cast out unclean spirits that caused convulsions, who healed the boy who threw himself into fire and water, who commanded the torment to leave and never return, and it obeyed instantly.

Lord Jesus, You still have that same authority right now. I believe You want me free from epilepsy and without medications controlling my life. I believe You want me to walk in full health, strength, and freedom so I can serve You and enjoy life with a clear mind and steady body.

I speak to this condition in Your authority: Seizures, **leave my body now!** Epilepsy, you have no right here! Every abnormal electrical discharge be silenced! Every risk of convulsion be nullified! My brain belongs to Jesus Christ, and it is healed, whole, and under His lordship.

In Your mighty name, I ask You to heal me completely. Stop all seizure activity. Stabilize every neuron, every synapse, every pathway in my brain. Restore perfect balance to my nervous system. Remove every trigger, every genetic related cause that has allowed epilepsy to take hold. Let my brain function exactly as You created it to function.

I thank You Father because I know You hear me. I thank You for the moment I realize weeks, months, years have passed with no episodes. I thank You for the testimony this healing will become.

In Jesus' name,

Amen.

Help My Unbelief!

Heavenly Father,

I come to You today carrying this struggle with unbelief. I want to trust You fully and believe Your promises are true for me. But honestly, part of me doubts. I've prayed before and not seen the answer. I've seen pain linger, doors stay closed, hopes disappointed, and it makes it hard to believe the next time I ask. My faith feels weak and unsteady, and I'm afraid my unbelief is blocking my prayers.

Lord, I confess this unbelief to You. Forgive me when I've let doubt grow bigger than Your Word and for every time I've questioned Your goodness. I repent of letting past disappointments harden my heart. I don't want to stay here. I want to believe.

Like the father who cried out to Jesus, I say: I believe, help my unbelief! Increase my faith. Strengthen what is weak. Replace doubt with certainty, fear with trust, questions with confidence in who You are. Show me Your faithfulness again so my heart can rest in You. Remind me of times You have come through.

Thank You that You do not despise my weak faith and You honor honest cries. Thank You that faith is Your gift, and You are the author and perfecter of it. Thank You that even a mustard seed of faith is enough to move mountains.

Renew my mind so faith grows stronger every day. Fill me with Your Holy Spirit who testifies to Your truth and builds confidence in my heart. When I pray, help me believe You are listening, moving, and working.

Thank You for meeting me in this honest place. Thank You for increasing my faith even now. I receive Your help and Your strength right now.

In Jesus' name,

Amen.

Spiritual Hosts of Wickedness in the Heavenly Places

FORBIDDEN OCCULT PRACTICES

"There shall not be found among you anyone who makes his son or his daughter pass through the fire, or one who practices witchcraft, or a soothsayer, or one who interprets omens, or a sorcerer, or one who conjures spells, or a medium, or a spiritist, or one who calls up the dead." (Deuteronomy 18:10-11)

"You are wearied in the multitude of your counsels; Let now the astrologers, the stargazers, and the monthly prognosticators stand up and save you from what shall come upon you. Behold, they shall be as stubble, the fire shall burn them; they shall not deliver themselves from the power of the flame." (Isaiah 47:13-14)

Forbidden Occult Practices

In the spiritual realm, malevolent forces often manifest through deceptive practices that draw humanity away from the one true God, enticing us with promises of hidden knowledge, power, or control. As believers, we must recognize that engaging in occult activities opens doors to these wicked influences. Throughout Scripture, the Lord declares such practices abominable, for they represent rebellion against His sovereignty and trust in created things rather than the Creator.

At the heart of God's condemnation of the occult lies witchcraft, a broad term encompassing sorcery, enchantments, and the manipulation of supernatural forces apart from Him. The Lord views these acts as detestable because they usurp His authority, seeking to harness powers that belong solely to the divine realm under His control. In the law given to Israel, God explicitly warns against such abominations, commanding that no one among His people should practice divination, sorcery, or witchcraft, for these defile the land and provoke His wrath.

Yet, the abomination persists today, often repackaged in modern forms such as Wicca or even seemingly benign practices like crystal healing or tarot readings. As believers, our response must be one of repentance and renunciation. If you have dabbled in witchcraft or been exposed to it, confess it before the Lord, claiming the blood of Jesus to cleanse and protect. Through such prayers, we dismantle the strongholds of these spiritual hosts, reclaiming heavenly places for God's glory.

Astrology is another occult practice that God deems abominable, though it often hides behind a veneer of innocence or intellectual curiosity. Astrology posits that the positions of stars, planets, and constellations influence human affairs, offering guidance through horoscopes, zodiac signs, and natal charts. Yet, Scripture condemns this as a form of divination, akin to witchcraft in its attempt to divine the future apart from God.

In Isaiah, the Lord declares that those weary from endless counsels and monthly forecasts will find no salvation in them; instead, they will be consumed like stubble in fire, unable to deliver even themselves. Deuteronomy 4:19 warns against being *"driven to worship them and serve them,"* referring to the sun, moon, and stars, which God has allotted to all peoples under heaven, but not for worship or divination. Astrology, by attributing destiny to the stars rather than to the Star-Maker, dishonors God and invites the influence of deceptive spirits. True wisdom comes from seeking the Lord alone, who holds the heavens in His hand and guides our paths with unfailing light.

Many today consult horoscopes, zodiac signs, or astrologers for guidance, dismissing it as harmless fun and unaware that this too is a form of divination rooted in ancient paganism. But the enemy uses it to erode faith, much like the Chaldeans who blended astronomy with occultism (Daniel 2:2-10). Daniel's refusal to consult such sources, instead turning to God for revelation, models our proper stance. The abomination is not in observing the beauty of the cosmos, but in perverting that glory into a system of false prophecy. Use the prayers that follow to renounce these abominations and claim victory over the hosts of wickedness through the name of Jesus.

FAMILIAR SPIRIT

*"And when they shall say unto you, Seek unto them that have **familiar spirits**, and unto wizards that peep, and that mutter: should not a people seek unto their God? For the living to the dead?"* (Isaiah 8:19, KJV)

Familiar Spirit[1]

A familiar spirit refers to a spirit or demon that a medium, necromancer, or wizard claims to consult for guidance, prophecy, or information about the dead. These spirits are depicted as being "familiar" in the sense of being known or controllable by the practitioner, sometimes manifesting as the ghosts of deceased relatives or loved ones to deceive or provide misleading insights. In biblical context, this practice is associated with divination, sorcery, and communicating with the dead, acts strongly condemned as idolatrous and contrary to seeking God directly.

Demons act as familiar spirits meaning they're acquainted with a person's history, habits, secrets, and relationships because they've monitored individuals or even entire families across generations. For instance, a familiar spirit might know intimate details like childhood nicknames, private conversations, or unresolved regrets that only the deceased would seemingly recall. In generational cases, these spirits attach to family lines, passing down knowledge of ancestors' lives, which enables them to impersonate multiple relatives convincingly.

The Bible indicates that Satan can *"disguise himself as an angel of light"* (2 Corinthians 11:14), and by extension, his demonic agents can transform or morph their appearance to imitate deceased loved ones. This includes visual manifestations, voices, or even sensory experiences like smells or touches that evoke the person.

In dreams, visions, or séances, they might appear as the loved one, sharing "messages" that align with what the living expect, such as comfort, warnings, or re-

---

1. Familiar Spirit (KJV, YLT)

   Mediums and Necromancers (ESV)

   Mediums and Wizards (NKJV)

   Spiritists (NASB, NIV, CSB)

   Spirits of the Dead (NLT)

quests. However, the Bible teaches that the dead cannot return or communicate (Ecclesiastes 9:5-6; Luke 16:19-31), so any such encounter is demonic imitation.

The primary goal of a familiar spirit is deception: to draw people into occult practices, foster false hope, or undermine faith in God. By acting like the deceased, these spirits exploit grief and curiosity, leading to spiritual defilement (Leviticus 20:6). They often reveal just enough truth mixed with lies to build trust, similar to how Satan twisted Scripture in tempting Jesus (Matthew 4:1-11). For example, a spirit might reference a shared memory accurately but then promote ideas like reincarnation that contradict biblical doctrine on death.

Familiar spirits don't have direct access to the souls of the dead, who, according to Scripture, are either with God or in judgment, unreachable by the living. Instead, they rely on pre-existing knowledge, supernatural mimicry, and psychological manipulation to create the illusion. The Bible urges testing spirits and avoiding all forms of mediumship or necromancy, as these open doors to demonic influence.

I Once Was a Minister of Satan

Heavenly Father,

I come to You in the name of Jesus Christ, my Lord and Savior. I confess that I have practiced witchcraft, seeking power or knowledge outside of You. I now recognize this as sin, rebellion, and idolatry. It opened doors to darkness, deceived me, and grieved Your Holy Spirit. I am truly sorry and repent with all my heart.

Lord, forgive me completely. Wash me clean by the blood of Jesus. I renounce and reject every involvement in witchcraft and the occult, every spell, incantation, curse, hex, spirit guide, familiar spirit, or demonic influence I ever engaged with or invited. I break and cancel any agreements, covenants, or ties made with darkness. In Jesus' name, I close every door I opened and command every evil spirit connected to this to **leave me now and never return!**

Thank You that there is no condemnation for those in Christ Jesus. Thank You that You are faithful and just to forgive my sins and cleanse me from all unrighteousness. Thank You that the blood of Jesus speaks a better word than any curse or spell.

Holy Spirit, fill me afresh. Renew my mind. Replace lies with Your truth, and guard my heart from any pull back to the old ways. If there are any lingering effects, break them by Your power. Surround me with Your angels and cover me with the armor of God. Help me live as Your child, free, forgiven, and fully surrendered to You.

Thank You for Your unfailing love and for welcoming me back. I receive Your forgiveness, cleansing, and freedom right now.

In Jesus' name,

Amen.

I Will Make No More Attempts to Contact the Dead

Heavenly Father,

I come to You in the name of Jesus Christ, confessing my sin with a broken and contrite heart. I have participated in seances, used Ouija boards, or engaged in any attempts to contact spirits, the dead, or other supernatural forces outside of You. I now see this clearly as rebellion against You, seeking knowledge, guidance, or connection from sources You forbid. It was sin, opening doors to deception and darkness, and I am truly sorry.

Lord, forgive me completely. Wash me clean by the blood of Jesus. I repent fully and turn away from these practices forever. I renounce every attempt to summon or communicate with spirits, mediums, or the dead, whether out of curiosity, fear, grief, or anything else. I break and cancel any spiritual ties, agreements, or influences I invited. In Jesus' name, I close every door I opened to darkness and command any evil spirits connected to this to leave and never return!

Thank You that You are merciful to those who repent. Thank You that the blood of Jesus breaks every curse, chain, and hold. Thank You that there is no condemnation for me in Christ, and that You remember my sins no more.

Holy Spirit, fill me now. Guard my heart and home. Help me trust only in You for guidance, comfort, and answers. Surround me with Your protection. If any effects remain, nightmares, or unusual feelings, deliver me fully by Your authority.

Draw me deeper into Your Word, prayer, and worship. Help me walk in obedience, free from the past. I choose life in You alone. Thank You for Your forgiveness, cleansing, and freedom. I receive it fully right now.

In Jesus' name,

Amen.

I Did Not Realize the Spiritual Implications of Yoga

Heavenly Father,

I come to You in humility today. When I practiced yoga, I truly believed it was nothing more than a healthy way to care for my body. I had no idea that many of the poses carry ancient spiritual meanings rooted in Hinduism and other Eastern spiritual traditions. I did not understand that I was unknowingly opening doors to harmful spiritual forces.

Lord, forgive me. I repent for participating in something that was designed to honor other gods. I confess that certain poses were created as offerings to Hindu deities, that mantras are invocations to spiritual beings, that "namaste" means bowing to the divine spark in another, and that the entire system was meant to prepare the body and mind for spiritual enlightenment apart from Jesus Christ.

I did not know these things at the time, but ignorance does not erase the spiritual reality. I may have opened myself up to unclean spirits, deceptive influences, false peace, or counterfeit spiritual experiences by participating in practices that belong to other spiritual kingdoms.

In the name of Jesus Christ, I renounce every door I opened through yoga. I break and cancel any spiritual tie, influence, agreement, or foothold that may have been established. I command every unclean spirit that entered through these practices to **leave me now!** You have no legal right here! I belong to Jesus!

Thank You Lord that You are merciful and understanding. From this day forward, I choose to honor You alone with my body, my breath, my mind, and my worship. Teach me healthy, neutral ways to care for my physical body that bring You glory and do not compromise my devotion to Jesus.

In Jesus' name,

Amen.

SPIRIT OF PYTHON

*"And it came to pass in our going on to prayer, a certain maid, having a **spirit of Python**, did meet us, who brought much employment to her masters by soothsaying, she having followed Paul and us, was crying, saying, 'These men are servants of the Most High God, who declare to us a way of salvation;' and this she was doing for many days, but Paul having been grieved, and having turned, said to the spirit, 'I command thee, in the name of Jesus Christ, to come forth from her;' and it came forth the same hour."* (Acts 16:16-18, YLT)

Spirit of Python[1]

Python refers to a massive mythical serpent or dragon in Greek lore slain by the god Apollo at Delphi, where he then established an oracle. The priestesses at this oracle, known as Pythia, would enter ecstatic trances to deliver prophecies and fortunes, often under the influence of vapors or rituals, serving as intermediaries for divine (or more accurately demonic) insights. By the time of the New Testament, "python" had become a cultural shorthand in the Greco-Roman world for a spirit or demon that enabled soothsaying, clairvoyance, or prophetic utterances, especially for profit.

From this verse in Acts, Paul, Silas, and others encounter a slave girl possessed by a spirit of divination. She followed them for days, shouting that they were servants of the Most High God proclaiming salvation. While the girl's declarations about Paul and his companions were technically true, they came from a demonic source, creating disruption likely intended to mock or undermine their gospel message.

Growing greatly annoyed, Paul finally stops, looks at the girl, and addresses not her but the evil spirit within her. With authority, he declares, *"In the name of Jesus Christ I command you to come out of her!"* This invokes the superior power of Christ over demonic forces. At that very moment, the spirit leaves her, freeing the girl from possession. She loses her fortune-telling abilities, which angers her owners and leads to Paul's arrest. This act exemplifies spiritual warfare: Paul's patience ends not in anger toward the girl but in bold, faith-filled action against the oppressing spirit.

---

1. Spirit by which she predicted the future (NIV, NLT, CSB)
   Spirit of Divination (KJV, NASB, NKJV, ESV)
   Spirit of Python (YLT)

I Renounce Tarot and All Forms of Divination

Heavenly Father,

I come to You today in humility and genuine sorrow. When I used tarot cards, practiced divination, read palms, cast runes, used pendulums, or engaged in any form of fortune-telling, I thought it was harmless entertainment. I did not understand that these practices are rooted in seeking knowledge, guidance, or control from sources other than You that can open doors to familiar spirits and forces that oppose Your truth. Lord, forgive me, I repent.

In the name and authority of Jesus, I renounce every form of divination, fortune-telling, tarot, mediumship, channeling, or occult practice I ever participated in. I break and close every spiritual door I opened, every agreement, every invitation, every tie to familiar spirits, deceiving entities, or demonic forces. I command every unclean spirit that entered through these practices to **leave me now!** You have no legal right here. The blood of Jesus has purchased me completely.

Father, wash me clean. Cleanse me from any lingering confusion, fear, false guilt, spiritual heaviness, nightmares, intrusive thoughts, or oppression that may have followed these activities. Fill every empty place with Your Holy Spirit, Your truth, Your peace, and Your light.

Thank You that You are merciful and compassionate. Thank You that when we come to You with a broken and contrite heart, You do not despise us. Thank You that no sin or mistake is beyond Your grace and cleansing.

From this day forward, I choose to seek You alone for direction. Teach me to trust Your Word, Your Spirit, and Your timing instead of looking to forbidden sources. I receive Your full forgiveness, complete cleansing, and total freedom right now.

In Jesus' name,

Amen.

I Turn Away From Astrology, Horoscopes, and Zodiac Signs

Heavenly Father,

I come to You today with an open and honest heart. When I read horoscopes, followed my zodiac sign, or used astrology for guidance, I truly thought it was harmless fun. I did not realize that astrology and horoscopes are rooted in ancient pagan practices that seek to divine the future, define identity, and gain knowledge from the stars and planets rather than from You, the Creator of those stars.

Lord, forgive me. I repent for looking to the created things for meaning instead of seeking You first. I confess that by reading and believing horoscopes I was unknowingly participating in divination and seeking guidance from false sources, opening doors to deceptive spirits.

In the name and authority of Jesus Christ, I renounce and reject every form of astrology, horoscope reading, zodiac identification, natal chart interpretation, transit predictions, or any occult use of the stars I ever engaged in. I break and close every spiritual door I opened, every agreement, every invitation, every tie to deceiving spirits, familiar spirits, or demonic forces that entered through these practices. I command every unclean spirit to **leave me now and never return!** You have no legal right here. The blood of Jesus has purchased me completely.

Father, wash me clean. Cover my mind, my emotions, my spirit, and my future with the blood of Jesus. Thank You that You are merciful and compassionate. Thank You that no practice or mistake is too big for Your grace to cover.

From this day forward, I choose to seek You alone for guidance. Help me walk in purity and obedience so no door is ever opened again.

I receive Your full forgiveness, complete cleansing, and total freedom right now.

In Jesus' name,

Amen.

Revival

Spirit of Uncleanness

*"And on that day, declares the Lord of hosts, I will cut off the names of the idols from the land, so that they shall be remembered no more. And also I will remove from the land the prophets and the **spirit of uncleanness.**"* (Zechariah 13:2, ESV)

Spirit of Uncleanness[1]

In the prophetic words of Zechariah, we glimpse a divine promise of purification and restoration, speaking directly to the heart of any nation entangled in spiritual defilement. In the biblical context, uncleanness refers to defilement that separates humanity from God's holiness with it's roots found in idolatry, false prophecy, and occult influences. It encompasses the overall effect demonic spirits have on a land and society. It is the residue of rebellion against the one true God. In our nation today, our land groans under this weight, much like ancient Israel experienced.

Yet, Zechariah's prophecy offers hope: a fountain opened for cleansing, a divine intervention that eradicates not just the symptoms but the root causes. If we, as a people of prayer and faith, rise to eradicate the false gods that grip our nation, then God Himself will act. He will cut off the names of these idols so they are remembered no more. He will silence the false prophets who peddle lies in the name of enlightenment. And crucially, He will remove the spirit of uncleanness from our land, washing away the defilement that has stained our collective soul. This is a supernatural purging, where the blood of Christ, the ultimate fountain of cleansing, flows to purify and renew.

Imagine a nation reborn if every prayer in this book was answered. As we intercede in prayer, binding these spirits and loosing the Holy Spirit's conviction, we position ourselves for this divine removal. Success in this spiritual warfare will usher in a season of revival, where uncleanness gives way to holiness, and our land becomes a beacon of God's glory.

But let us heed the solemn warning woven into this promise. Rebuilding after such a cleansing will not be without struggle. Our nation may lie in tatters,

---

1. Spirit of Impurity (NIV, NLT)

   Spirit of Uncleanness (YLT, ESV)

   Unclean Spirit (KJV, NASB, NKJV, CSB)

economically strained, socially divided, culturally disoriented, as the old strongholds crumble. In these vulnerable moments, we must be vigilant. Jesus Himself cautioned in Matthew 12:43-45 about the unclean spirit that, once cast out, wanders and returns to find the house empty, swept, and put in order. It then brings seven spirits more wicked than itself, making the final state worse than the first. So it could be with us. If we expel these influences but fail to fill the void with the fullness of God's presence, the door swings open for a greater invasion.

As we conclude this prayer book, let us commit to this path of perseverance. May our prayers not cease at victory but continue as the guardians of renewal. Let us pray together:

Heavenly Father,

We thank You for the fountain of cleansing opened through Your Son, Jesus Christ. As we labor to eradicate the false gods, deceptions, and occult strongholds in our nation, remove the spirit of uncleanness from our land. Grant us wisdom in the rebuilding, that we may fill every emptied space with Your Holy Spirit. Guard us from complacency, lest worse evils return. Restore our nation to holiness, for Your glory alone.

In Jesus' name we pray,
Amen.

May this vision propel us forward, a people cleansed and consecrated, until the day when every knee bows and every tongue confesses that Jesus Christ is Lord.

Prayer to Seek Out Idols in My Life

Heavenly Father,

You know me completely, every thought, motive, and desire. I come before You humbly, not trusting in my own self-awareness, because I know my heart can deceive me.

Like David prayed, I ask: *"Search me, O God, and know my heart. Try me and know my thoughts. And see if there is any grievous way in me."* (Psalm 139:23, ESV)

Expose hidden idols in my life:

- Any place I seek security, identity, comfort, or worth apart from Christ,

- Any relationship, achievement, possession, or habit that has taken Your rightful place,

- Any bitterness, unforgiveness, or control I cling to instead of trusting You, and

- Any area where I've made good things into ultimate things.

Holy Spirit, shine Your light into the dark corners of my heart. Convict me where I've been blind or complacent. Give me courage to name what You reveal. Help me confess it fully to You, turn away from it, and destroy its hold on my life. Replace every false god with deeper love for You.

Thank You, Lord, that You are faithful and just and have already forgiven my sins. Thank You that nothing can separate me from Your love in Christ Jesus. Lead me in the way everlasting. Restore to me the joy of Your salvation.

In Jesus' name,

Amen.

Father, Please Renew My Mind

Heavenly Father,

I come to You in the name of Jesus Christ, my Savior. You know my heart better than I do. You see every thought, motive, and hidden corner where sin still lingers. I confess that my mind has been shaped by the world, by old habits, by lies I've believed, and by my own selfish desires. I have not thought like You, and my ways have been wicked in Your sight.

I repent right now of ____________. I turn from these wicked ways. Forgive me through the blood of Jesus. Wash me clean and create in me a clean heart. Renew a right spirit within me.

Holy Spirit, I ask You to renew my mind today. Transform my thinking according to Your Word. Be renewed in the spirit of my mind. Replace lies with Your truth. Help me take every thought captive to obey Christ. Fill my mind with what is true, honorable, just, pure, lovely, commendable, excellent, and praiseworthy. Give me the mind of Christ.

Strengthen me to reject conformity to this world and to pursue Your perfect will. Let Your peace guard my heart and mind in Christ Jesus. Day by day, make me new inwardly, even as outward things fade.

Thank You, Father, that You are faithful and just to forgive my sins and to cleanse me from all unrighteousness. Thank You for Your mercy that is new every morning. Thank You that in Christ I am a new creation; the old has gone, the new has come.

Help me walk in this renewal. Lead me in paths of righteousness for Your name's sake. Draw me closer to You so my thoughts, words, and actions glorify You.

In Jesus' name,

Amen.

Fill Me With the Holy Spirit

Heavenly Father,

I come to You in the name of Jesus Christ, my Savior and Lord. Thank You that I belong to You, that I have been born again, sealed, and indwelt by Your Holy Spirit. Yet I recognize my constant need to be under His full influence and control.

Lord, as Your Word commands in Ephesians 5:18, I ask You right now: Fill me afresh with Your Holy Spirit. Holy Spirit, come and take complete control of my life today:

- Fill every part of me, my mind, heart, will, emotions, body, and actions,

- Convict me of any sin or resistance that hinders Your work,

- Empower me to walk in obedience, to resist temptation, and to live out Your fruit in my character,

- Guide me into all truth, give me wisdom for decisions, boldness to share Christ, and love for others, and

- Stir up the gifts You've placed in me for Your glory and the good of others.

I surrender my plans, my pride, my fears, and my self-effort. I yield the throne of my life to You. Have Your way in me. Lead, direct, strengthen, and use me however You desire. Thank You, Father, for Your promise to give the Holy Spirit to those who ask. Thank You for hearing me and for the fresh infilling I receive by faith. I praise You, Holy Spirit, for Your presence and power. Fill me to overflowing so that my life overflows with Your love, joy, peace, and glory to God.

In Jesus' name,

Amen.

Heal Our Land

Heavenly Father,

You have promised that if Your people humble themselves, pray, seek Your face, and turn from their wicked ways, You will hear from heaven, forgive our sin, and heal our land. We come humbly before You today, confessing our nation's worship of false gods and principalities that have infiltrated our nation, leading us astray from Your truth. We confess that as individuals and as Your church, we have too often placed our trust in human systems, leaders, wealth, and power rather than in You alone, and we ask for Your forgiveness in this reliance on worldly things.

Lord, we pray against the spiritual strongholds that grip our nation. We repent for the failures of Your church, including our compromises with the world and silence on matters that reflect Your heart. Grant us the strength to stand firm and break these chains through Your power, as we war against these forces in Your name.

We thank You, gracious God, for Your boundless mercy that covers our shortcomings, for Your past faithfulness that has sustained us through trials, and for the gospel that brings hope and redemption to all. Ignite a spiritual awakening in our midst. Revive the hearts of believers and draw the lost into salvation through Your Son. In this time of need, we trust in Your sovereignty to bring renewal and unity, healing our land as we align our lives with Your will.

In Jesus' name we pray,

Amen.

Other Biblical Spirits

JUDICIAL SPIRITS

There are judicial spirits in the Bible that God sent in times of judgment. These are different than demonic spirits as they are controlled by God. A brief overview is provided to understand how they are different than all other spirits in this prayer book.

Spirit of Perverseness[1]

*"Jehovah hath mingled in her midst A **spirit of perverseness**, And they have caused Egypt to err in all its work, As a drunkard erreth in his vomit."* (Isaiah 19:14, YLT)

God sent a spirit of perverseness as an act of divine judgment of Egypt. Rather than sending an invading army, God sovereignly pours this spirit into the nation so that its leaders and people become completely disoriented. Every plan fails, every decision collapses, and the once-proud empire staggers *"as a drunken man staggers in his vomit"* (KJV). The perverseness here is not moral perversion but a profound twisting of the mind and will that renders wise men foolish and strong men helpless.

This spirit is not portrayed as a roaming demonic entity that Christians must cast out of individuals. It is a specific instrument of God's judgment, used at a particular moment in history to bring down a powerful nation that had trusted in its own gods and wisdom instead of the Lord. In short, the biblical spirit of perverseness is divine judgment in the form of mental and moral confusion, a reminder that when people persistently reject God's truth, He can withdraw clarity and leave them staggering in their own foolishness.

---

1. Perverse Spirit (KJV, NKJV)

   Spirit of Confusion (ESV, CSB)

   Spirit of Distortion (NASB)

   Spirit of Dizziness (NIV)

   Spirit of Foolishness (NLT)

   Spirit of Perverseness (YLT)

Spirit of Sadness[2]

*"And the Spirit of Jehovah turned aside from Saul, and a **spirit
of sadness** from Jehovah terrified him; and the servants of Saul
say unto him, 'Lo, we pray thee, a spirit of sadness [from] God is
terrifying thee.'"* (1 Samuel 16:14-15, YLT)

The context of this verse regards Saul being rejected as king for his disobedience (1 Samuel 15). At that very moment the Holy Spirit departed from him and God actively sent a spirit of sadness to come upon him as divine judgment. The result was deep terror, emotional torment, depression, and later violent rages that made Saul unstable and dangerous.

Unlike New Testament accounts of demonic possession, this spirit is not portrayed as an independent demon roaming the earth. It is explicitly *"from Jehovah"* and functions as an instrument of God's righteous judgment on a king who had rejected His word. The same God who removed His empowering Spirit also sent this distressing spirit to trouble Saul's mind and heart. It is a historical example of how God can sovereignly withdraw His peace and allow torment as discipline upon those who persistently disobey Him. David's harp music temporarily soothed Saul (1 Samuel 16:23), pointing forward to the greater peace that only the true King can bring.

---

2. Distressing Spirit (NKJV)

   Evil Spirit (KJV, NASB, NIV, CSB)

   Harmful Spirit (ESV)

   Spirit of Sadness (YLT)

   Tormenting Spirit (NLT)

Spirit of Falsehood[3]

*"And he saith, 'Therefore, hear a word of Jehovah; I have seen Jehovah sitting on His throne, and all the host of the heavens standing by Him, on His right and on His left; and Jehovah saith, Who doth entice Ahab, and he doth go up and fall in Ramoth-Gilead? and this one saith thus, and that one is saying thus. And the spirit goeth out, and standeth before Jehovah, and saith, 'I -- I do entice him'; and Jehovah saith unto him, 'By what?' and he saith, 'I go out, and have been a **spirit of falsehood** in the mouth of all his prophets;' and He saith, 'Thou dost entice, and also thou art able; go out and do so.' And now, lo, Jehovah hath put a **spirit of falsehood** in the mouth of all these thy prophets, and Jehovah hath spoken concerning thee -- evil."*
(1 Kings 22:19-23, YLT)

In this passage, the prophet Micaiah describes a heavenly vision in which the Lord is seated on His throne surrounded by the host of heaven. God asks who will entice King Ahab to go up to Ramoth-Gilead so that he will fall in battle. A spirit steps forward and volunteers. The Lord approves the plan, and the spirit is sent. As a result, all 400 of Ahab's prophets speak lies with one voice, promising victory when defeat is certain. The text explicitly states that *"Jehovah hath put a spirit of falsehood in the mouth of all these thy prophets"* as judgment upon Ahab.

This is not a rogue demon acting independently; it is a spirit dispatched by God Himself as an instrument of divine judgment. Ahab had rejected the true word of the Lord and surrounded himself with flattering false prophets who told him what he wanted to hear. In response, God sovereignly sends a deceiving spirit to

---

3. Deceiving Spirit (NASB, NIV)
   Lying Spirit (KJV, NKJV, NLT, ESV, CSB)
   Spirit of Falsehood (YLT)

ensure that the deception is complete, leading the rebellious king to his death. This passage illustrates a recurring biblical theme: when people persistently reject God's truth and prefer lies, the Lord can withdraw clarity and actively permit or send a spirit of falsehood to seal their delusion (see also 2 Thessalonians 2:11).

Spirit of Deep Sleep[4]

*"For the Lord has poured out on you the **spirit of deep sleep**, and has closed your eyes, namely, the prophets; and He has covered your heads, namely, the seers."* (Isaiah 29:10)

God is pronouncing judgment on Jerusalem for its hypocrisy; the people honor Him with their lips while their hearts are far from Him (verse 13). As an act of divine judgment, the Lord sovereignly *"pours out"* this spirit of deep sleep upon the nation, causing a profound spiritual lethargy and blindness. The prophets and seers, whose eyes should have been open to God's revelation, are now spiritually asleep; their vision is shut and their heads are covered, rendering them unable to understand or declare the true word of the Lord.

This spirit is not a roaming demon that possesses individuals at random. Rather, it is a specific instrument of God's righteous judgment, sent to produce insensibility and stupor in a people who have willfully rejected His truth. He sends a spirit of deep sleep to confirm the spiritual numbness that the people have already chosen. The result is a nation that staggers in spiritual darkness, unable to perceive God's hand or hear His voice. It's a sovereign act of judgment from God upon a hypocritical nation, underscoring the sobering reality that persistent rejection of God can lead to a divinely imposed inability to awaken.

---

4. Brought over you a deep sleep (NIV)

An overwhelming urge to sleep (CSB)

Spirit of Deep Sleep (KJV, YLT, NASB, NKJV, NLT, ESV)

Evil Spirit[5]

*"And God sent an **evil spirit** between Abimelech and the leaders of Shechem, and the leaders of Shechem dealt treacherously with Abimelech, that the violence done to the seventy sons of Jerubbaal might come, and their blood be laid on Abimelech their brother, who killed them, and on the men of Shechem, who strengthened his hands to kill his brothers."* (Judges 9:23-24, ESV)

God actively sent an evil spirit to stir up division, mistrust, and betrayal between Abimelech and the leaders of Shechem who had once supported him. The result is treachery and civil strife that ultimately destroys both parties. This is not God creating evil or tempting with sin (James 1:13 affirms God does not tempt anyone to evil), but rather God withdrawing protection, permitting demonic activity, or actively dispatching such spirits to execute righteous judgment on those who have persistently rebelled against Him. This fits a pattern of judicial or punitive action, where God uses secondary causes (including evil spirits) to bring consequences for sin.

The passage makes the purpose clear: the spirit's work ensures that the bloodguilt of Abimelech's massacre of his seventy brothers (Judges 9:5) is repaid in full. Abimelech, who seized power through murder and ambition, and the men of Shechem, who endorsed his crime for personal gain, now turn on each other in mutual destruction. The evil spirit functions as God's judicial agent, provoking the discord that brings righteous retribution upon both the perpetrator and his accomplices. This account underscores a recurring biblical theme: when people

---

5. Evil Spirit (KJV, YLT, NASB, ESV, CSB)
   Spirit of Ill Will (NKJV)
   Stirred up animosity (NIV)
   Stirred up trouble (NLT)

commit grave injustice and shed innocent blood, God can sovereignly permit or send an evil spirit to sow division and execute judgment, ensuring that violence returns upon those who practice it.

JEZEBEL

*"Now therefore, send and gather all Israel to me on Mount Carmel, the four hundred and fifty prophets of Baal, and the four hundred prophets of Asherah, who eat at **Jezebel's** table."* (1 Kings 18:19)

Jezebel[1]

Jezebel was a Phoenician princess who married Ahab, king of the northern kingdom of Israel. Her marriage was a political alliance, and she was involved in occult practices and practiced sorcery. Within years she had installed hundreds of prophets of Baal and Ashtaroth at the royal table, erected temples to them across the land, and launched a systematic purge of God's prophets.

Her contempt for the God of Israel reached its peak in her deadly feud with the prophet Elijah. After Elijah's triumph on Mount Carmel, Jezebel swore to take his life before the next sunset, forcing the prophet to flee for his life.

Her most notorious crime was the judicial murder of Naboth. When Ahab sulked over Naboth's refusal to sell his ancestral vineyard, Jezebel arranged false witnesses, orchestrated a sham trial for blasphemy, and had the innocent man stoned to death so the king could seize the property. For this act of royal theft and bloodshed, the prophet Elijah pronounced the doom of Ahab's entire house: every male descendant would be cut off, and Jezebel herself would be eaten by dogs.

The prophecy was fulfilled with brutal precision. Years later, during the bloody revolution led by the soldier Jehu, Jezebel stood at an upper window and taunted the usurper. At Jehu's command, her own eunuchs threw her down. Her body was trampled by horses and left in the street; by the time men came to bury her, only her skull, feet, and the palms of her hands remained.

In the centuries that followed, her name became synonymous with seductive evil, religious corruption, and feminine power turned against God. Even in the New Testament, the risen Christ warns the church in Thyatira against *that woman Jezebel* (Revelation 2:20) who teaches God's servants to practice immorality

---

1. Jezebel (KJV, YLT, NASB, NIV, NKJV, NLT, ESV, CSB)

and eat food sacrificed to idols, proof that her shadow still lingered wherever compromise with paganism threatened the faith of Israel.

We often hear about a Jezebel spirit but this isn't in the Bible. When you hear someone say a Jezebel spirit, they are describing someone acting in the character or manner of Jezebel. She was a real person not an evil spirit. Her behaviors however were influenced by demonic forces.

LEVIATHAN

*"In that day the Lord with His severe sword, great and strong, Will punish **Leviathan** the fleeing serpent, **Leviathan** that twisted serpent; And He will slay the reptile that is in the sea."* (Isaiah 27:1)

"On earth there is nothing like him, Which is made without fear. He beholds every high thing; He is king over all the children of pride." (Job 41:33-34)

Leviathan[1]

Leviathan is not a man or a demon, but the ultimate sea monster, a twisting, fire-breathing dragon that no human weapon can subdue.

The longest and most vivid portrait appears in Job 41, where God Himself describes Leviathan to a humbled Job. Its scales are like rows of shields, tightly sealed; its mouth rings with terrible teeth; its sneezes flash forth light and its eyes are like the dawn. When it rises, the mighty are terrified. Spears, arrows, and swords are useless against it. Smoke pours from its nostrils, flames leap from its mouth, and its heart is as hard as stone. *"He is king over all the children of pride,"* God declares (Job 41:34).

Elsewhere the Bible calls it *"the twisted serpent"* and *"the reptile that is in the sea"* (Isaiah 27:1). In Psalm 74:14, God crushes Leviathan's heads and feeds its carcass to the wilderness creatures. In Psalm 104:26, the same creature frolics in the ocean like a playful pet formed by God's own hand.

Ancient readers understood Leviathan as a primeval forces of chaos that threatened to swallow creation. To the prophets, it could represent Egypt or Babylon, monstrous powers that God would one day slay with His *"severe sword, great and strong"* (Isaiah 27:1).

The Bible's final word on Leviathan is hope, not horror. Isaiah promises that on the day of the Lord, this ancient serpent will be punished and destroyed. What no man can tame, the Creator will end forever. Leviathan stands as the Bible's supreme emblem of untamable power, however it does not state there is an actual Leviathan spirit. Instead, Leviathan as a symbol or type that points toward Satan, especially through connections to serpents, dragons, chaos, and pride.

---

1. Leviathan (KJV, YLT, NASB, NIV, NKJV, NLT, ESV, CSB)